Praise for *The Politics of Education: A Critical Introduction*

"Educating our citizens is a political act, and if teachers are not familiar with how political thought influences them and the system in which they work, they will be buffeted by forces they do not understand and cannot control. This informative book provides insights teachers need. A must-read for the concerned educator."

—**David Berliner,** Regents Professor Emeritus, Arizona State University

"Saltman's engaging text provides the reader with the critical tools to make sense of the current politics of education. Readers are introduced to complicated concepts in ways that show how they help us deconstruct the dominant discourses and practices. Furthermore, the writings of both well-known and unfortunately neglected theorists are put into context so that their usefulness becomes clear. Highly recommended for the beginning and advanced student of education policy!"

—**David Hursh,** University of Rochester

"Teachers need this book because Kenneth Saltman shatters the deep conviction that their work has nothing to do with politics. Each chapter opens up another part of the unacknowledged political imperatives that define the schoolroom—from critical pedagogy as a meaning-making practice to cultural imperialism to what corporate school reform is really about. I needed this book for my first fifteen years as a teacher."

—**Susan Ohanian,** teacher, educational activist, and author of *Why Is Corporate America Bashing Our Schools?*

Critical Introductions in Education

Kenneth J. Saltman, Series Editor

Titles in the Series

The Politics of Education: A Critical Introduction
By Kenneth J. Saltman (2014)

Forthcoming in the Series

Math Education: A Critical Introduction
By Mark Wolfmeyer

Teaching English Critically
By Philip Kovacs

Social Studies Education: A Critical Introduction
By E. Wayne Ross

Teaching Science Critically
By Clayton Pierce

The Politics of Education

A Critical Introduction

Kenneth J. Saltman

Paradigm Publishers
Boulder • London

Published in the United States by Paradigm Publishers, 5589 Arapahoe Avenue, Boulder, Colorado 80303 USA.

Paradigm Publishers is the trade name of Birkenkamp & Company, LLC, Dean Birkenkamp, President and Publisher.

Library of Congress Cataloging-in-Publication Data

Saltman, Kenneth J., 1969–
The politics of education : a critical introduction / Kenneth J. Saltman.
pages cm
Includes bibliographical references and index.
ISBN 978-1-61205-443-8 (pbk. : alk. paper)
ISBN 978-1-61205-590-9 (eBook)
1. Education—Political aspects. 2. Education and state. I. Title.
LC71.S234 2013
379—dc23

2013022451

Printed and bound in the United States of America on acid-free paper that meets the standards of the American National Standard for Permanence of Paper for Printed Library Materials.

Designed and Typeset by Straight Creek Bookmakers.

18 17 16 15 14 1 2 3 4 5

Contents

Series Preface

The Politics of Education is the first book in the Critical Introductions series with Paradigm Publishers. Books in the series provide critical introductions to social studies education, math education, English education, science education, art education, educational leadership, and more. The series is designed to offer students who are new to these subjects an introduction and overview—a first book for a first course. These "primers" covering the key subjects of education are intended to help students broadly comprehend their new field socially and politically. While primers in the series engage with dominant liberal and conservative views on subjects, they ask readers to comprehend dominant perspectives of a subject area through a critical lens that focuses on social justice, power, politics, ethics, and history. Additionally, these volumes provide students with a new vocabulary and key framing concepts with which to interpret future knowledge about the field gleaned through academic study and clinical experiences in schools. For this reason Critical Introductions include boldfaced key terms in the text that are defined in a glossary in the back. They also include lists of suggested readings and potential questions for discussion with each chapter. The books are suited for instructors to pair chapters with selections from the lists of suggested readings at the end of each chapter.

Ideally these Critical Introductions can both be a kind of field guide or handbook arming students to interpret experiences in schools and also serve as a foundational text for future deeper scholarly study and development of a critical understanding of educational subjects built through further engagement with newly acquainted authors and texts. Critical Introductions also offer a basis for social and political engagement and possibly activism within the field of education because they ground their examinations of particular subjects in terms of broader contemporary school policy and reform debates and struggles. In this sense, even advanced graduate students and seasoned scholars in education would benefit from consulting these Critical Introductions for a fuller comprehension of their field and the political struggles and stakes in several subjects affecting teachers, students, and colleagues.

This book, *The Politics of Education: A Critical Introduction*, provides an introduction and overview to numerous dimensions of the politics of education with reference throughout to contemporary educational reform and restructuring debates. The book gives the reader an understanding of the views of the politics of education coming from different political perspectives. It distinguishes between accommodationist and socially transformational approaches to comprehending the social roles and function of schooling. It addresses politics from broad social, systemic, institutional, and structural vantage points, linking these broader realities to the individual, local, and practical realities of schooling and the possibilities of student and teacher agency and collective struggle.

Part of what makes *The Politics of Education: A Critical Introduction* new and unique is the way that it brings together so many different aspects of politics and a variety of critical perspectives: cultural politics, political economy, hegemony theory, globalization, neoliberalism, class, gender, race, biopolitics, disciplinary power, psychology, "the commons." And it manages to address numerous contemporary policy issues including but not limited to curriculum, pedagogy, privatization, common core, standardized testing, school funding, single-sex education, racism in schooling, and global organizations and their local impacts. Finally, it is unique for doing all this while introducing a variety of critical theoretical perspectives including critical theory, critical pedagogy, psychoanalysis, feminism, and Foucauldianism in an accessible way.

Acknowledgments

This series was developed collaboratively with the education editor at Paradigm Publishers, Jason Barry. His extensive ideas for the format and key features of the book and the series have been extremely valuable and formative. I want to express my gratitude to both Jason and Dean Birkenkamp for being such a pleasure to work with on this and other Paradigm projects.

Two friends went above and beyond to help me improve this book. Robin Truth Goodman read, edited, and made crucial suggestions on every chapter of this book. She is a wonderful collaborator and friend not to mention a brilliant scholar. I can't thank her enough for her invaluable help. I am also enormously grateful to Alex Means who took time from finishing his brilliant book *Schooling in the Age of Austerity* to do extensive editing and make significant suggestions for the first half of the manuscript that resulted in reorganization, rewriting, and major improvements to entire chapters. Additionally, I thank David Hursh who reviewed the manuscript for publication and made valuable editorial suggestions.

I want to thank a number of friends and colleagues who provided ongoing exchange that informed the work in various ways including Henry Giroux, Susan Giroux, Enora Brown, Stephen Haymes, Amira Proweller, Mark Garrison, David Gabbard, Wayne Ross, Philip Kovacs, Julia Hall, Sheila Macrine, Joao Paraskeva, Alex Molnar, Sarah Hainds, Karen Lewis, Stephen Ball, Kristen Buras, Pauline Lipman, Noah De Lissovoy, Donaldo Macedo, Jeffrey DiLeo, Clayton Peirce, Graham Slater, Noah Gelfand, and Kevin Bunka.

I would like to thank the University Research Council at DePaul University for providing a paid leave grant that supported this project in fall quarter 2012 with a release from three courses of my seven-course annual teaching load.

Introduction
What Are the "Politics" in the Politics of Education?

Liberal, Conservative, and Critical Perspectives on the Politics of Education

> This chapter explains a number of different perspectives on the politics of education, discusses how education is inevitably political, and maps the differences between a number of liberal, conservative, and critical approaches on the politics of education as they relate to curriculum, pedagogy, policy, and administration. It explains how the common claim that education is apolitical or just a matter of practical technique is itself a political claim. Lastly it gives a chapter forecast and explains the organization of the book.

This book provides an introduction to the politics of education. In the last few years, political fights over education have become highly visible in the popular press and mass media. Some of the most publicized educational "reforms" for K–12 have included charter schooling (the private management of public schools), reducing teacher tenure, paying teachers for student test scores and not for experience and advanced degrees, limiting the power of teachers to collectively bargain in a union and reducing their ability to strike, expanding vouchers (that allow public tax dollars to pay for private, for profit, and religious schooling), expanding scholarship tax credits for private schooling (encouraging parents to opt out of public schools and to receive public funding to attend private schools), standardizing a common core curriculum, and linking public funding to student test scores. This seemingly disparate collection of reforms actually follows a very consistent pattern that understanding the politics of education helps us to grasp.

The pattern of these reforms, however, cannot be understood by looking to the commonplace political categories of the mainstream electoral political parties. Republicans and Democrats, as much as they disagree over a number of issues, have become increasingly aligned when it comes to changing education. Both parties have largely come to embrace what critics, including myself, have described alternately as "corporate school reform," "neoliberal education," or "market-based school reform." That is, both U.S. political parties have come to view public schooling from the perspective of the values, interests, and rationales of the owners and managers of businesses. The central concern has come to be how schools can prepare future workers for businesses and how such workforce preparation can set the stage for "winning" global economic competition among nations.

As well, schools and districts have come to be increasingly modeled on corporate culture. Administrators are described as "CEOs," teachers need to "deliver" numerically measurable results, students are dressed in uniforms resembling business attire or retail uniforms, curriculum and pedagogy are increasingly standardized, and schools must "compete" against each other for test scores to secure federal funding while parents are described as "consumers," as if public schools are private services. To younger readers, such market-oriented assumptions about the purposes and role of education may seem so commonplace and obvious that they don't seem worthy of question. Nor do they appear to be particularly about politics. However, these educational values are relatively recent, quite radical, and thoroughly political. They have in the last two decades steadily supplanted other long-standing values such as education for the making of the full human being, education for political participation and civic engagement, and education for what educational philosopher **John Dewey** called social reconstruction—that is, learning to reinterpret experience in order to remake the social world and its institutions. In the current climate the idea of the efficient delivery of knowledge, the measurement of such delivery through standardized testing, and the standardization of teaching and curriculum have taken central importance. Perhaps the single most significant difference in the turn toward the business view of schooling is how it imagines public schools as being primarily for the benefit of individual students or families rather than the whole society. Society is only invoked as benefitting individuals as workers and consumers rather than as human beings or citizens.

The now dominant business view of knowledge and teaching presumes that education is not inherently political, that the principle educational problems involve methodological approaches to delivery of so-called content knowledge. Subjects such as English, math, science, and social studies in this view are seen as politically neutral or should be treated as politically neutral for most students at most ages despite the fact that different individuals, cultural groups, and economic classes do not agree as to how these subjects should be taught or what counts as important to teach. For example, should students learn to memorize literary texts as they have in the past? Should students learn national literature? The literature of "silenced voices" such as women writers, workers, and immigrants? Should they learn analysis of literature in terms of form emphasizing character, plot, and conflict? Should they learn to interpret texts in terms of ideologies and related material interests? With science as an example, should students memorize formulas? Should learning focus on conceptual understanding? Should students learn religious alternative explanations to science or even religious explanations of the natural world in the place of or alongside scientific ones? Should the teaching of science and math be done through the lens of social problems and issues rather than in decontextualized ways? The fact is that people do not agree about the answers to these questions. Nor are such disagreements merely intellectual. However, the disagreements are hardly random. Understanding the patterns of such disagreements requires a deeper understanding of how competing visions for education enact and reflect competing visions about the social world and further the interests of particular groups.

These disagreements about the social purposes and roles of schooling are another way of thinking about the politics of education. Such consideration moves us beyond the limited conceptual tools offered by political parties. Such contestation over values, ideas, ideologies, and material interests gets us closer to understanding the sea change in educational policy and practice in the last decade in the United States.

In what follows here I break down the politics of education into three basic categories about the social purposes of education: conservative, liberal, and critical. Following this discussion, I describe the chapters that follow. Each chapter builds on and expands what is meant by the politics of education.

The Social Purposes of Education: Three Political Views

Both liberal and conservative perspectives on education share a view that schooling plays a crucial role in maintaining society, preparing individuals for participation in the existing economic and political systems, or at least allowing the individual an opportunity to compete for access to dominant institutions such as the workforce and the political system. Liberals and conservatives also largely agree that more schooling translates to more opportunity for inclusion and that schooling creates workers for the nation's economy so that the nation can compete successfully against other nations for markets and jobs in a capitalist economy. Another way to describe what the liberal and conservative perspectives share is to say that they aim for education to transmit dominant values, knowledge, and dispositions (though they may not agree completely as to what these values are), and they assume that such transmission is beneficial to the individual and the society as a whole.

We might term this an **accommodationist** perspective because schooling is thought to accommodate the student to the existing social order. Where the liberals and conservatives disagree is on how best to transmit or deliver dominant values, knowledge, and dispositions. They also disagree to some extent about which values, knowledge, and dispositions should be emphasized. (I take this up in greater detail in the next chapter on cultural politics of education.) They also tend to disagree about pedagogical approaches and curriculum. As we will see, this shared commitment of the liberals and conservatives to accommodating the individual to the existing social order stands in stark contrast with the critical or radical approach to schooling, which sees schooling as, on the one hand, serving to reproduce existing unjust social structures and yet, on the other hand, having the potential to transform this unjust social order toward a more just, equal, free, and democratic arrangement of structures, institutions, and practices.

Liberal View of the Politics of Education

Liberal education can refer to either the liberal philosophical tradition that has its origins with the European **Enlightenment** or to a set of views associated with **political liberalism** (as represented by Hobbes, Locke, etc.). In reality, the conservative, critical, and liberal political perspectives all emerge from philosophical liberalism with its emphasis on the use of reason, the possibilities for human emancipation, and progress. Contemporary political liberals tend to also put a premium value on the possibilities for education to be apolitical, politically neutral, or nonideological.

As well, drawing on the philosophical liberal tradition, contemporary educational liberals value education for its perceived role in the making of social consensus. Most liberals emphasize pedagogical approaches that involve liberal forms of communication such as dialogue, debate, and **critical thinking** or problem-solving skills. They presume that the classroom format and kind of communication fostered in it models the liberal political values of a democratic society. However, these pedagogical values conflict with another value common to liberals: the emphasis on the effective delivery of allegedly neutral content. Hence, liberals tend to be willing to entertain experimentation with pedagogical approaches and methodologies that are deemed effective, and they are open to experimentation with methodologies that promise more "effective delivery." The liberal framing of promoting educational methods that "work" have a loaded assumption about what such methods work to do. Typically, liberals have come to accept the formerly conservative measure that what works should be measured by standardized test scores. Such experiments with "what works" in the current climate tend to be market-based experiments and tend to take a form at odds with the liberal emphasis on dialogue, debate, and critical thinking because they instead emphasize standardization, enforcement of knowledge, and delivery.

Liberals usually call for equal distribution of educational resources such as school spending in order to expand access. In the liberal view, if there were more access to educational resources, then there would be a more level playing field for individuals to compete for social opportunities. As Stanley Aronowitz has suggested, even the progressive tradition of John Dewey accepts the ideal of access for schooling, which accepts class inequality as a social inevitability rather than seeing schooling as a means to contribute to genuine economic equality in terms of wealth, income, and control over industry. In other words, liberals do not see schooling as wrapped up with a project to end economic inequality. Rather they presume class inequality as a given and put the burden on individuals to fight for opportunity.

The liberal view represents upward mobility for individuals as taking place on a relatively level playing field despite the fact that, within the current economic, political, and cultural structures, there is extreme social inertia for continued inequality. Class positions in the United States are largely transferred generationally, even more so than in all other industrialized nations. Exclusionary access to political power follows the economic inequality in the United States as vast sums of money are required to buy media-driven election campaigns, which ensures that political candidates will keep within the views, assumptions, and interests of large donors and for-profit media companies that run ads.

Liberals have typically criticized efforts for the federal defunding of education such as those under President Ronald Reagan while having made little effort toward truly equal educational funding. Such an effort at equalizing funding would involve, for example, following the example of the rest of the industrialized nations and federalizing and equalizing educational spending. Instead, most liberals have taken as unfair but unchangeable the current system in which educational funding comes from local real estate taxes and hence is yoked to class status. In the existing system about 70 percent of funding comes through local taxes, 20 percent through state, and less than 10 percent through federal funding. A result has been the maintenance of a class- and race-segregated system in which those (predominantly professional-class whites) who can move to well-funded schools, in suburbs or rich parts of cities, do. In predominantly white working-class rural areas, this arrangement has also resulted in low levels of educational funding.

During the 1960s and 1970s, liberals sought racial equality for education by supporting busing and racial equity magnet schemes. By the 1980s the political will and aspiration for bold solutions to racial segregation in public schooling had largely collapsed. By the 1990s many liberals began turning toward or acquiescing to market-based remedies and market-oriented framings of educational problems championed by fiscal conservatives, including a willingness to embrace charter schooling and public-private partnerships. While liberals have historically been leery of reducing the quality of education to that which is only numerically measurable through test scores, by the 1990s many liberals had come to accept conservative descriptions of educational problems that naturalized test scores as the rightful measure of educational quality.

For example, liberals now largely accept that there is an "achievement gap" that can be measured in different test scores by different racial and ethnic groups. The achievement gap presumes that the norms of knowledge measured by tests, which are in fact class and cultural group specific (largely white and professional class), should be understood as universally valuable. Here again liberals in education espouse contradictory views regarding educational values: they emphasize the value on the humanities, critical thinking, and dialogue, but they have come to accept framings of educational value in ways that reduce understanding to decontextualized claims, reduce learning to that which is measurable, and replace dialogue and thought with memorization and test preparation. The acceptance of such framing has been unequally applied by liberals who have insisted on the retention of liberal values and have resisted standardization and teaching to the test in the predominantly richer, whiter schools and yet have accepted rigid, scripted enforcement-oriented approaches for poor, working-class, and nonwhite schools and communities.

This disparity is seen in glaring detail in the approaches taken by the charter operators (such as KIPP) and for-profit management companies (like Edison Learning) running schools in urban areas. Employing rigid and disciplinarian-style pedagogies of control, charters are heralded as spectacular successes despite test scores that are on par with or worse than the abysmal levels typical in these districts, and despite the emphasis on approaches, which Henry Giroux has characterized as a prohibition on thinking.

Working-class and poor families—especially African Americans and Latinos who are overrepresented among the poor and working class—have been historically shortchanged by the public school system and particularly by the funding inequalities, racial and ethnic segregation, and repressive pedagogical approaches. Meanwhile, professional class whites in suburbs have benefited from the seldom-acknowledged unequal arrangement that captures public tax money in order to maintain in their own neighborhoods world-class facilities organized around liberal values. Many minorities and the poor have soured on the public system and are understandably unreceptive to the liberal arguments for defending traditional neighborhood public schooling in the face of the current privatization trend for chartering and vouchers. The unequal historical arrangement is indefensible. Criticalists contend that any defense of public schooling must be grounded in remaking the system in ways that are truly equal in terms of funding, racial integration, and critical educational practices that aim for equality and justice outside of schools.

The liberal-accommodationist perspective fails to recognize the political, economic, and cultural antagonisms that constitute the social order. For example, liberals seldom acknowledge that owners of industry and workers in those industries have contradictory economic interests in a capitalist economy. Owners need to cut pay, benefits, and taxes on profits to maximize profits and compete with other businesses. Workers desire and need higher pay, benefits, and other supports (education, child care, health care, etc.) that can only come at the expense of owner profits. These different groups have antagonistic interests and ideas about what the public school system should do for them. The centrality of the liberal value on consensus over antagonism does not allow for serious understanding of what is at stake in the political battles over education.

Many people coming from the perspective of business are concerned foremost with training future workers. They want students to be educated (at public expense) at the level appropriate to that workforce and to learn to be docile and disciplined workers who won't revolt, strike, and make demands on owners and who will understand the world through the eyes of the owners. Through this type of accommodationist education, students learn to see political issues through the perspective of groups (like owners) that have interests contrary to their own. Because most liberals accept the framing of education for individual and national economic competition, few liberals have any way of addressing incommensurable economic interests and the educational values that correspond to these interests. Such is the case with the global race to the bottom for cheap labor. One of the most highly regarded liberal educational policy scholars, Linda Darling-Hammond, who was President Barack Obama's campaign education advisor for his 2008 campaign, is particularly revealing in her confusion about the relationship between education and the economy. She argues that the United States should have greater equality of distribution of educational resources so that it can compete with other nations for scarce jobs. She even says that the United States should do this so that it doesn't "fall like Rome." Here the liberal vision of greater educational access meets its dire limitations. In reality, are U.S. students preparing to compete against cheap and highly exploited Chinese labor to do industrial production in sweatshops? Should U.S. students accept the assumption that being an empire with military bases ringing the globe to ensure the supply of cheap consumer goods is a desirable or ethical vision for the future? Do advertising-driven manufactured desires in the "knowledge economy" have any relationship to meaningful shared values or the crisis of environmental stewardship facing the nation and planet? The current system of schooling prepares students to do collective labor for of the individualized benefit for those who own and manage institutions. Surely a more egalitarian working arrangement can be imagined and schooling can prepare students for it.

The liberal view also comes up against intractable problems in terms of the reality of politics in the contemporary United States. In the liberal view, education is intended to produce students who understand their citizenship rights. This in turn should ensure access to electoral politics. But our current system doesn't allow equal access; the possibility of elected office at most higher levels of government is largely limited to those with vast wealth who can buy political advertising and campaign public relations strategists. In addition to the corporate capture of politics, the significant curtailing of civil liberties in the first decade of the new millennium under the "war on terror" scaled back freedoms including privacy, speech, right to congregate and protest; limited habeas corpus; and allowed for targeted assassinations of U.S. citizens. The liberal promise of schooling for political access and civic participation has no way of addressing the basic exclusions of political democracy for large and growing numbers of citizens nor of dealing with the enormous recent changes to the political scene in the last few years. These changes are so extreme that a number of scholars, public intellectuals, and journalists ranging from Chris Hedges to Sheldon Wolin to Henry Giroux have described the United States as being on the cusp of a totalitarian corporate state with an increasingly privatized repressive control system. The liberal approach to education presumes a more or less level playing field but fails to comprehend that no such thing exists: different classes and cultural groups struggle for control of both the political system and public education, and these competing classes have widely varying amounts of political, economic, and cultural power.

In a cultural sense, liberals see the value of schooling as not merely molding workers and consumers and preparing students for civic participation. They also see schooling as a means for individuals to develop as enlightened human beings, to inherit the cultural wealth of liberal traditions of thought and creativity, and to learn creative, thoughtful, and rational approaches to knowledge from a variety of traditions including the sciences and arts. For this reason many liberals oppose the efforts of fiscal conservatives (a group also known as **neoliberals**) to reduce schooling to vocational training, to implement a narrow, back-to-basics curriculum, and to teach to tests—all tendencies within the corporate school model. But the liberal view is limited by its understanding of culture as disinterested and neutral that can be captured in a canon. Liberals may value multiculturalism, but cultural difference is often treated as an add-on to the cultural canon, something peripheral and only important because of the political value on inclusiveness or on market-based assumptions about serving changing demographic populations. Liberalism ignores how culture is interwoven with class struggles and how symbolic values are wrapped up with material struggles. And while the liberal perspective emphasizes critical thinking as a problem-solving skill, it ignores the **cultural politics of education**—that is, the extent to which knowledge represents the interests and ideological perspectives of particular classes and cultural groups and the extent to which knowledge and schooling itself are struggled over to win cultural dominance and claim universality.

Conservative Views of the Politics of Education

Education conservatives break down broadly into two main categories: **fiscal conservatives** and **cultural conservatives**. Fiscal conservatives (also known as **neoliberals, market fundamentalists**, and **corporate school reformers**) tend to justify education predominantly through an economic lens. This is the dominant perspective today and one that has been taken on not only by many Republicans but also by the conservative wing of the Democratic Party, which has dominated the party since Clinton and the ascendancy of the conservative Democratic Leadership Council. Fiscal conservatives see schooling as primarily for molding workers and consumers. Fiscal conservatives understand public schools as private services and treat parents as consumers who shop for schools. As well, fiscal conservatives treat teachers as private service providers who deliver a commodity to students. Administrators in this vision are imagined as business managers.

The fiscal conservative view corresponds to a broader **neoliberal** economic perspective and ideology emphasizing privatization and government deregulation of private markets. Most fiscal conservatives see public schooling as a problem because of the very fact that it is public. They believe education is a private consumable service that can be shopped for measuring cost against quality and that can be improved the way business people attempt to improve businesses—by squeezing more productivity out of the labor force while imposing cost-cutting and efficiency measures.

Despite the fact that public schools are "producing" educated people rather than profits and primarily serve the public rather than private owners, fiscal conservatives tend to treat knowledge as ideally measurable, and educational progress is likened to cash or commodities. Hence, they emphasize the centrality of standardization and standardized testing to measure progress. Schools are imagined like factories and the aim is to streamline production to speed up efficiencies. It is no wonder that fiscal conservatives promote efforts to weaken or destroy teachers' unions as a threat to greater delivery efficiency and to reduce costs despite evidence that this results in a less-experienced teacher workforce and higher rates of teacher turnover.

In reality, the corporate school reforms that have been promoted in the past fifteen years, including privatization, chartering, vouchers, contracting, turnarounds, and urban portfolio districts, have not proven to be better than traditional public schooling even as measured by the criteria of their conservative proponents—increasing test scores and decreasing costs. Liberals and criticalists see the failure of these reforms as much more serious. For liberals, the reforms have made numerical shell games the centerpiece of educational policy and have narrowed the curriculum to that which is testable at the expense of a well-rounded curriculum in the liberal arts and civic engagement. For criticalists, the reforms have made a dogma out of markets at the expense of a critical curriculum in which questions of knowledge are taken up in relation to power, politics, history, and ethics. However, because criticalists from the political left were the harshest critics of public schooling—because of its tendency to reproduce and exacerbate broader social inequalities through unequal funding, racial segregation, and an anticritical bent—criticalists are in a difficult position to defend public schools in response to fiscal conservatism and efforts to privatize education.

If fiscal conservatives make money the measure of education (and everything else), then cultural conservatives make conservative moral values its measure. Education is intended to socialize young people in accordance with traditional value codes, including proper submission to authority. Sometimes these codes are grounded in religion such as the Ten Commandments, and sometimes they are grounded in virtue ethics, such as character education, and to be found in the classics. Culturally conservative education emphasizes memorization, submission to authority, and a hierarchical view of culture and knowledge.

E. D. Hirsch is one of the most well-known cultural conservatives in education. He has spent his career promoting a "common core" of knowledge, based on the traditional Western canon, that every student should know. Another well-known cultural conservative is former secretary of education William Bennett, who wrote a number of books on traditional virtues. Bennett was a conservative celebrity for many years, but his star has waned in the wake of several scandals, including revelation of a gambling addiction and his statement that he opposes abortion even though the crime rate would be lowered if more black fetuses were aborted. Bennett's arguably unvirtuous behavior suggests more than just hypocrisy; it raises questions about the limitations of the cultural conservative emphasis on educating for individual character or individual submission to moral codes.

Cultural conservatives tend to emphasize curriculum and pedagogical approaches heavy on respect for and oftentimes obedience to authority and dominant traditions and respect for the government or at least the authoritarian parts of it. This dogmatic view emphasizes the value of the canon without exploring how individual works became canonical. It fails to explore how traditional texts and traditions have bolstered the views and interests of the powerful or how those same texts have been sometimes interpreted in ways that promote the views and interests of nondominant groups. Cultural conservatives tend to support unquestioning faith in capitalism yet will subjugate questions of profits to their version of moral or religious values.

In the current climate of corporate school reform, cultural conservatives and fiscal conservatives find a natural affinity despite different emphases. The fiscal conservative emphasis on schooling that is measurable and quantifiable finds that cultural conservatism provides content, the canon of knowledge, to make measurable and quantifiable. The intersecting interests of cultural conservatives and fiscal conservatives are clearly illustrated by the largest company (in terms of student enrollment) that is managing schools for profit. That company, K12, Inc., runs virtual charter schools and online homeschooling. K12, Inc., was founded and is partly owned by the aforementioned William Bennett and E. D. Hirsch and promotes the common core curriculum of the cultural conservatives. These educational management organizations profit by collecting public tax money (a set amount per pupil) and then spending less on teachers, staff, materials, and other overhead so that the difference can be taken out to financially benefit the owners.

While fiscal conservatives or neoliberals have a vision of eradicating public schooling by redefining it as a private service, cultural and religious conservatives often attack public schooling as an institution, framing it as a manifestation of government tyranny. Conservative politicians such as Rick Santorum have recently sought to win votes by describing public schooling as "government schools" to suggest that public funding for education is tantamount to totalitarian state intervention into private life. In this view, schooling is the domain of the private family and private religious faith. Both of these conservative anti-public perspectives, while accepted by many working-class people, benefit those with the greatest financial resources and cultural power.

Critical Perspective on the Politics of Education

The critical perspective on education is different from both the liberal and the conservative perspectives in several ways. While liberals and conservatives conceive of culture as a series of texts and knowledge to be passed on to new generations, critical pedagogy emphasizes culture as a matter of the unequal exchange of meanings through meaning-making practices. In the view of critical pedagogy, all meaning-making practices need to be scrutinized for the kinds of authority they secure, the sorts of social relationships they foster, and the material and symbolic interests they affirm or contest. While in the view of critical pedagogy, culture is inherently political and struggled over, for cultural conservatives culture is closer to dogma.

The critical view of virtue is different as well. While cultural conservatives put the greatest emphasis on individual codes of conduct despite different circumstances, critical pedagogy emphasizes the importance of social context in the moral choices that people make. Choices, in this view, are never made in a vacuum. Put the most ethical, well-intentioned person in an unethical or desperate institution or context and he or she will inevitably be in a position to make unethical choices that he or she would never make in a more supportive context. The point not to be missed is that culture is formative of **social character** from which individual character is forged and in which individual actions are made meaningful. Critical pedagogy emphasizes teaching for individuals to be **agents** to act with others to make more just and moral social contexts for everybody.

Criticalists have long held complex views about the role of public schooling. On the one hand, schooling is seen to have reproduced existing inequalities including class hierarchy and cultural symbolic meanings that privilege some groups and individuals while disadvantaging others. On the other hand, schooling has also been part of the struggle to challenge historical inequalities. Schools can be democratic **public spheres** that can foster critical consciousness, democratic dispositions, and habits of engaged citizenry. They can play a crucial role in producing subject positions, identifications, and social relations that can make radically democratic subjects committed to such projects as democratizing the economy, strengthening the public roles of the state, challenging oppressive institutions and practices, and participating in democratic culture. As well, from a critical perspective, knowledge is subject to interrogation in relation to relations of power, questions of politics, history, and ethics. Experience needs to be problematized and theorized in relation to broader social, cultural, and political struggles, forces, and realities informing experience.

The critical perspective is also distinguished by its emphasis on theory. The liberal, cultural conservative, and fiscal conservative perspectives on education tend to devalue the necessity for students and teachers to have the theoretical tools to interpret their experiences in schools and outside of schools. Criticalists make the theoretical tools of interpretation a starting point for teachers and students to interpret individual and social reality as the basis for community and collective social intervention. For criticalists, **theory** always undergirds practices. The field of education has long suffered from an antipathy to theory. Educational reformers, policy wonks, and many teachers have accepted a false understanding in which theory does not matter to teaching and school reform because what really matters is educational practice. Practicalism can be found among liberals and conservatives who tell us that all that really matters is figuring out the right methods for practice, or all that really matters in improving schools is discovering and implementing the practical reform strategy, and so on. Practicalism infuses the language of educational leaders who speak of needing to codify "best practices" and it dominates the culture of some schools with talk of good teaching coming from experience "in the trenches" and not through educational study, teacher education programs, or educational theory. The issue is not whether or not theory matters but whether or not individuals develop the capacity to understand the values, assumptions, ideas, and ideologies behind practices. Theory is indispensable for interpretation of and reflection about practices. In the critical perspective, such critical examination of subjective experience in relation to objective forces ideally becomes the basis for **agency** and action directed at transforming oppressive forces and structures. The understanding of the need for practice to be theorized and for theory to become the basis for new forms of action on the world is known as **praxis** and is developed by a number of critical educational thinkers including **Paulo Freire**, **Antonio Gramsci**, and **Henry Giroux**, among others. Critical education also challenges the assumption that educational and social justice can be achieved within the frame of one nation-state. Instead, critical education looks to the ways that economic production and exploitation are global in nature, that politics and citizenship must be conceptualized in global terms, and that with global media and the postcolonial and imperial situations, culture, too, must be thought globally.

From the critical perspective, the denial of the politics of education ought to be understood as political. When liberals insist that we should all come to consensus about knowledge, curriculum, and pedagogy, or when conservatives insist that we can canonize the knowledge of the best and brightest and reduce teaching to methods, these denials of the politics of education serve those groups who benefit from consensus, serve those whose knowledge has been elevated, and serve those who replace education as a process of questioning with education as a process of consumption of dogma. The denial of politics of education denies that both education and society are dynamic and changing rather than static. The question is, how will institutions, social arrangements, and meanings change, and *who* will change them, and *why*? The denial of the politics of education shuts down these questions, which are utterly crucial for any aspirations for just, equal, and free social and educational change.

Forecast

Each of the following chapters take up a different aspect of the politics of education to deepen and expand upon the contested views about schooling and its purpose discussed above and to link these discussions to contemporary matters of policy and practices.

Chapter One explains the concept of cultural politics with reference to the work of Paulo Freire, Stuart Hall, Henry Giroux, Antonio Gramsci, Raymond Williams, Pierre Bourdieu, and others and explains what is at stake in the denial of cultural politics. It discusses knowledge as canonical versus contested. It explains these ideas through current trends toward standardization of the curriculum, standardized testing, and the liberal declaration of the end to the "curriculum wars."

Chapter Two begins by explaining what is meant by "political economy" and then examines how the ownership and control of schooling matters in terms of public interests and values, the cultural politics of the curriculum, and the reproduction of a class hierarchy. What is the difference between public and private control of schools and curriculum? How does the ownership and control of schools relate to economic formations and relationships throughout the society? Can schooling be imagined as the basis for a more just egalitarian economic arrangement that democratizes economic relationships and undermines social hierarchies?

Drawing predominantly on Erich Fromm, Paulo Freire, Michel Foucault, Slavoj Zizek, and feminist education scholars informed by psychoanalysis, Chapter Three considers ego psychology and poststructuralist psychology as alternatives to the dominant psychological strains of educational psychology and human development. The chapter uses the critical psychology approaches to problematize depoliticized versions of educational psychology and highlights the assets and limitations of humanist and poststructuralist critical perspectives in terms of policy and practice. The discussion distinguishes character education from the pedagogical making of what Fromm calls social character and challenges psychological theories that deny the possibility for the pedagogical formation of critical consciousness.

Chapter Four elaborates the hegemony theory of Antonio Gramsci and the class reproduction theories of Louis Althusser and Pierre Bourdieu and discusses the shift away from these theories in the last two decades, especially in terms of the influence of Foucault's conception of power and the cultural turn in education toward identity politics and multiculturalism. It contends that reproduction theory needs to be revived in ways that do not suffer theoretical pitfalls regarding structure and agency.

Chapter Five explains Michel Foucault's concepts of disciplinary power and normalization and uses them to analyze contemporary trends in standardized testing, the making of students into cases studies, and the differential making of racialized subjects through school discipline, the idea of the "achievement gap", and racially segregated corporate school reform.

Chapter Six discusses the different versions of biopolitics (or regulatory power) as the production and management of populations and the management of life and death. It looks at the making of disposable populations inside and outside of schools, the culture of control throughout education, lifelong learning, and the ways that the increasing corporate control over education invades the body and the body politic.

Chapter Seven explains how neoliberalism as ideology and economic doctrine is a form of class warfare and market sovereignty that has been restructuring educational policy and practice for thirty years. It details how neoliberalism is a radical politics that has rapidly undermined liberal and cultural conservative perspectives on schooling while threatening the possibility for the formation of critical forms of education.

Chapter Eight discusses gender in recent educational reform policies by taking on the material and symbolic war on women. It draws on Judith Butler's theory of performative subject formation and discusses the different ways that feminist pedagogy and critical pedagogy address the problem of gender inequality in schooling and society.

Chapter Nine discusses the current direction of the politics of education on a global scale. It focuses on how the neoliberal approach to school restructuring is being applied internationally and how that perspective is being promoted by transnational organizations, nongovernmental organizations, and corporate philanthropies. It suggests the limitations of nationally based politics of education that are incompatible with any theory of just education.

Chapter Ten brings recent literature on "the commons" to bear on public schooling, drawing on the original common school movement of Horace Mann, which founded the public school system, and also drawing on recent literature in the humanities on the commons. Literature on the commons offers a way of thinking about the politics of education in terms of the expansion or enclosure of the common labor of the teacher, student, and administrator. According to a number of scholars associated with the autonomist movement, advanced capitalism has at its core knowledge-making and subjectivity-producing activity. This chapter considers how different forms of public and private control over schooling produce the common or enclose it. The chapter suggests reinventing the traditional common school movement in order to create the conditions for collective forms of living and working throughout the society.

The Organization of This Primer

The chapters in this book begin with an abstract describing what the chapter does. While chapters do build upon prior chapters in terms of what is assumed of the readers, the chapters each stand on their own and can be taught in any order at all. Chapters also include boldfaced key terms that are defined in the glossary in the back. Each chapter after this one also contains a list of suggested readings from which the chapter draws and that allows the reader further investigation and deeper study. As well as offering possible teaching text in beginning graduate studies or undergraduate courses, these suggested readings lists serve as potential reading companions for each chapter. Each chapter ends with some questions for reflection and possible discussion.

Suggested Further Reading

Kenneth J. Saltman. *The Failure of Corporate School Reform*. Boulder, CO: Paradigm, 2012.

Questions for Discussion

1. What are some of the key assumptions of the conservative views of public schooling, and how do these appear as policy?
2. What are some of the key assumptions behind the liberal views of public schooling, and how do these appear as policy?
3. What are some of the key aspects of the critical view of public schooling, and what do they suggest about policy and practice?

Chapter One
The Cultural Politics of Education

> This chapter contrasts the liberal and conservative versions of cultural politics of education with a critical one by explaining the concept of cultural politics with reference to the work of Paulo Freire, Stuart Hall, Pierre Bourdieu, and Henry Giroux, among others, and explains what is at stake in the denial of cultural politics in terms of an understanding of knowledge as canonical versus contested. It explains these ideas through current trends toward standardization of the curriculum, standardized testing, and struggles over the so-called curriculum wars.

The Introduction distinguished between conservative, liberal, and critical versions of the politics of education, drawing a broad distinction between the socially transformative aims of the critical approach and the social accommodationist aims of both the liberal and conservative perspectives. The **cultural politics of education** can be understood through a similar matrix. Both the liberal and conservative perspectives see culture in the tradition of Matthew Arnold as a collection of the "best and brightest" of human endeavors—ideas and art. Education in this accommodationist view is centrally about *transmitting* this thing called culture to the young.

These issues came to a head in the so-called **culture wars** of the 1980s and 1990s, which largely focused on education. During this time period, conservatives like Allan Bloom and E. D. Hirsch pushed back against what they saw as liberal trends in education. Although both liberals and conservatives believed in culture as a set of canonical texts to be transmitted, liberals had begun to advocate for expanding the canon to include works by historically marginalized cultural groups including women, African Americans, and Latinos. Conservatives pushed back by stridently defending a curriculum based on the "great books" of Eurocentric tradition. In books like Hirsch's *Cultural Literacy* they likewise defended traditional interpretations of historical events that had recently begun to be reexamined from a multicultural perspective.

Criticalists took yet a third approach. Like liberals, they embraced multiculturalism but also sought to promote a view of culture as inherently political, highly contested, and interwoven with class interests and power struggles; Donaldo Macedo's *Literacies of Power: What Americans Are Not Allowed to Know* represents one of the finest efforts to expound this view and offers a critical counterpunch to Hirsch's *Cultural Literacy.* Like conservatives, they saw culture as politically contested but sought to question the Western tradition rather than simply reproduce it. For many cultural conservatives, the preservation of cultural values or rather "purity" and avoidance of cultural "decadence" is of primary value. In this view the cultural traditions of the past must be enshrined and defended. For criticalists the cultural traditions of the past are no more sacred than the cultural practices of the present, and all must be subject to interrogation in terms of whose interests and perspectives they represent. For example, while criticalists see numerous values in a classical text such as Plato's *Republic,* they also see it as requiring interpretation in terms of the authoritarian values it promotes, the social relationships it suggests, and the way that the social and individual values relate to contemporary public problems.

Many criticalists want to take all forms of cultural production seriously in terms of how they function pedagogically and politically. Consequently, not only should a classical work of philosophy be taken seriously but so should hip hop music, which mobilizes the desires, stimulates the interests, and speaks to the dreams of many people today. The point is not that these cultural works are equal or need to be hierarchically ranked in terms of their cultural importance or classified into categories of "high" and "low." The critical perspective shifts the question altogether to a primary focus on what cultural works *do* as the products of meaning-making practices and processes. This is the political question of culture: what do cultural products do? The poetic question of culture asks what cultural works *mean.* When we ask what cultural works *do,* we are asking how their meanings affirm or contest already existing sets of meanings (or

discourses), how in a given context a cultural work tends to have what Stuart Hall calls a **preferred meaning** yet how this preferred meaning is never finally fixed, and how such preferred meanings mobilize people to act in the material world.

Today there is another wave of push-back against critical tendencies. Liberal experts in education such as Linda Darling-Hammond feel that it is time for liberals and everybody else to "get over the **curriculum wars**." Even Diane Ravitch, who has come to defend public schooling against privatization, declares the need to get past the curriculum wars. Ravitch retains cultural conservative values, positioning privatization as a threat to the "strong curriculum" that can be codified through common core standards. Other liberals such as Jonathan Kozol, Mike Rose, Richard Rothstein, and Richard Kahlenberg advocate against privatization and excessive testing.

But all of these thinkers, liberal and conservative alike, advocate essentially the same thing: better practices, more rigor, essentially carrying on the educational practices of the past but simply doing a better job of it. They make arguments for "strengthening" public schooling (avoiding privatization, stopping the overemphasis on testing) while ignoring what criticalists consider to be the most crucial dimension of public schooling: cultural politics.

Cultural Politics: Stuart Hall's Constructivist Theory of Culture

Cultural politics is at the heart of the critical perspective on education. The concept emerged in the field of cultural studies. One of the leading figures in that field was **Stuart Hall**, who argued that culture is about shared meanings that are produced through dialogue, albeit always in unequal exchanges. In Hall's perspective, for a sign, a representation, or a practice to become meaningful, there must be a shared understanding about it. However, meanings change. Hall challenges the idea of cultural meanings as being inherent in a text, a sign, or an object that transcends time and space. Signs, symbols, and representations do not speak for themselves. They require interpretations and the interpretations become meaningful in particular contexts. Cultural politics is the struggle to make meaning among competing parties and a recognition of the inevitable meaning-making dimensions of human practices.

We can see how meaning is context-specific through the examples of some well-known symbols. A swastika in contemporary U.S. culture is largely seen as being a symbol of the Nazis. It evokes the sadism of the Nazis in World War II, the horrors of the Holocaust, and the ongoing threat of neo-Nazism around the world. However, prior to the 1920s when the Nazis made it their symbol, the swastika was associated with American Indians, Hinduism, and Buddhism and carried none of the connotations of racism and oppression that is has since garnered. In fact, if one travels to countries that are predominantly Hindu or Buddhist one can still find the swastika displayed as an ancient symbol related to those religions. Stuart Hall uses the example of the British flag, the Union Jack. The Union Jack was traditionally displayed alongside white people and became a symbol of white "Englishness." Now it can be seen waved by black athletes in international competitions, and its meaning is reworked. It suggests not only Englishness but the relationship between race, global competition, and excellence, among other commonly linked meanings that are tied to the flag.

Stuart Hall rejects cultural meaning as being fixed, universal, and timeless. He also rejects an understanding of cultural meaning as the result of authorial intention. Just because an author writes something with a meaning in mind or a director makes a film with a meaning in mind, how the book or film will be interpreted cannot be strictly determined or assured. Instead, communities of interpretation make sense of the cultural product. Hall calls this **preferred readings**—interpretations that are likely at a particular time and place as opposed to fixed for all time. There is an indeterminacy at the core of signs, symbols, images, and representations. This indeterminacy of meanings leaves open the possibility for people to make different interpretations and for the meanings of representations to change and be changed. In fact, for Hall we are, all the time, involved in meaning-making practices, what he calls **signifying practices**. These signifying practices include not only language but everything that we do that becomes meaningful or "signifies" in a community.

Cultural Politics and the "Responsible" Teacher

Hall's ideas on culture are highly significant for teachers as cultural workers. Cultural workers are those people who are engaged in public meaning-making activities, and teachers are key public figures in the making of meaning for young people. Teachers inevitably make pedagogical choices. When they choose a curriculum, plan lessons, and teach, then teachers become responsible for what meanings they make in the classroom. We can think of "responsibility" in three ways here.

First, teachers are always responding to already existing broader public discourses. That is, they are entering a context in which there are already existing ideas, values, and ideologies about a whole range of things from nation, gender, and race to leisure, science, and nature, to name but a few broader public discourses. Teachers are responding by affirming or contesting existing broader public discourses in what they say, write, and do.

Second, teachers are also responsible for the ethical and political implications of what they knowingly or unwittingly affirm or contest in schools and classrooms. Their meaning-making has both school-based and broader social implications, which is why educational theorist Paulo Freire emphasizes **praxis**—the ongoing process of reflecting on and theorizing one's experiences and actions. As Henry Giroux explains, the issue is not whether or not teachers' practices are based in theories; rather, it is the extent to which teachers understand what theoretical underpinnings and assumptions are behind their practices.

A third sense of teacher responsibility holds teachers in a relationship of responding to students and the social contexts inhabited by teachers and students such that teaching and learning is understood as being dialogic and driven by the exchange of meanings. Teachers are responsible for taking seriously the subjective experiences and histories that students bring to the pedagogical encounter. They are also responsible for helping students to interpret those experiences in terms of the social context and social forces that inform and produce those experiences. Through dialogue and the exchange of meanings between teachers and students, the subjective experiences of both can be understood as produced by broader objective conditions. Moreover, through dialogue, subjective experiences and particular contexts can be interpreted as a means of shaping and transforming the objective social conditions and future experiences.

The responsibilities of teachers in these three senses are all related to an awareness of cultural politics. They differ radically from the transmission-oriented idea of teacher responsibility that holds teachers responsible for delivering knowledge that experts elsewhere deem of most value. In that disciplinary idea of teacher responsibility, teachers must simply enforce the right knowledge.

Cultural Politics and Class: Pierre Bourdieu and the Forms of Capital

If cultural politics is the process of meaning-making among competing parties, who are these parties that compete for cultural meaning? Sociologist **Pierre Bourdieu** believed that economic class was a critical category in the competition for cultural meaning. He offered important insights into the three ways that class privilege is transmitted from generation to generation.

The first way that class privilege is transmitted is through money, the traditional meaning of the word **capital**. Parents bequeath financial wealth to their children in several ways. They purchase elite private schooling, allow them to attend cultural events, make investments, and simply give them money. All of these things constitute a form of heritable privilege.

A second way that class privilege is transmitted is through **social capital**. Social capital refers to the social networks that individuals are able to join that allow for social benefit. For example, parents who are members of the wealthy professional class share social networks that give them advantages that those outside their network don't enjoy. They exchange knowledge of how to gain entry into prestigious schools. They share tips on how to take advantage of public resources. Their alumni status may give their children a leg up on admission to universities. And university graduates themselves enter the social networks of alumni associations, which may transform into real capital in the form of coveted jobs and connections to gain capital. In all of these cases, knowing other people of privilege translates into privilege for oneself and one's children. Social capital is, in effect, the people one knows.

The third way in which privilege is transmitted is through **cultural capital**. Cultural capital refers to the knowledge, tastes, and dispositions that are socially valued and rewarded and the tools for appropriating them. Bourdieu distinguished between objectified, embodied, and institutionalized forms of cultural capital. Objectified forms of cultural capital are physical objects like works of art or books. Embodied forms of cultural capital are not physical but intellectual: possessing the tastes and opinions that are rewarded in society. Institutional forms of cultural capital refers to institutional recognition like college degrees, board certifications, and the like. Again, the possession of all of these forms of cultural capital results in continued privileges for the possessor.

Cultural capital for Bourdieu begins in the home and is rewarded or punished in the schools. For example, an infant with parents from the professional class is regularly read to at home. The infant learns familiarity with language but also learns that reading and books are familiar, that books are something that mother and father value, and so on. When this child arrives at school, she already has a particular disposition toward book learning, understands the book as being important, associates it with familial care. Right from the beginning, the school rewards this "second nature" disposition that the child has toward the book. The working-class or poor student who is unfamiliar with books from the beginning is at a disadvantage in an institution that rewards book learning. Such unfamiliarity may then be the basis for the student being subjected to a series of sorting and sifting techniques. Some may be as simple as observation: the teacher notices that some students demonstrate interest in books and others don't. These dispositions become the basis for mistakenly naturalizing as intelligence or diligence what are in fact differently distributed forms of cultural capital. Likewise, students of professional parents may be more comfortable with test-taking. Tests demand of professional class students much of what they already know and find second nature to come to know, while the same tests demand of working-class and poor students what they do not know and find alien to come to know.

Perhaps the working-class or culturally subordinate child has even learned implicitly or explicitly that books are associated with a culture of power from which the child is excluded. Bourdieu terms this experience of having one's culture, knowledge, language, tastes, and dispositions devalued "**symbolic violence**." Symbolic violence is not only an external force on individuals but also involves the student internalizing the "rules of the game." So, for example, after a short time of being in the school dominated by professional-class knowledge, tastes, and dispositions, the working-class student learns to judge herself as inferior, lazy, and unintelligent and learns that what she gets is her own "just desserts." The student is thus made complicit in her own cultural oppression. This is a cultural oppression that has material effects: the sorting and sifting techniques of the school such as testing are used to position students to do different work and to have different things.

Bourdieu's insights are extremely valuable for comprehending how culture, language, knowledge, and curriculum are made and valued in ways that correspond to the economic class hierarchy and its maintenance. However, culture ought not be understood as merely about domination and economic determinism. Individuals and groups, teachers and students, mediate, interpret, and resist dominant meanings. In fact, there is a sizable critical educational tradition of studying how students do resist oppressive culture, including work by Paul Willis, Henry Giroux, Dick Hebdige, Nadine Dolby, and others.

Willis in *Learning to Labor*, for example, shows that subcultural groups within a school can resist class oppression in schools but that usually such resistance becomes the basis for students to learn to become complicit in their own class subjugation in the workplace. Henry Giroux's book *Theory and Resistance in Education* distinguishes between student acts of opposition (simple defiance of authority) and acts of resistance in which opposition to authority aims to challenge and address oppressive forces in the institution. Giroux asks how teachers might identify acts of student resistance and make them the basis for comprehending with students what they are experiencing, what produces those experiences beyond the self, what social and institutional forces are involved in making those experiences, and ultimately how a different understanding of resistance for the student can become the basis for social and political agency for the student to work with others to transform the social forces that produce the original experience of oppression. Giroux's book is important for theorizing how teachers as engaged in cultural politics are not merely agents for reproducing the oppression of the school but can also become agents involved in producing hopefully more emancipatory meanings, understandings, and actions with students.

Implications for Contemporary Educational Policy

The fact that culture is struggled over by different individuals and groups in schools and other educative institutions matters for the kind of future world that teachers and students work to create. A basic difference between the critical educational perspective and that of the liberal and conservative ones is that criticalists see the meaning-making practices of teaching and learning as the basis for the future of human values, human work, human leisure, what science should be pursued, and to what ends. As well, criticalists see knowledge and curriculum holistically as inextricably linked to the broader world outside of schools.

In the past two decades, educational reform has come to be dominated by **positivist ideology**. Positivism, sometimes referred to as radical empiricism or objectivism, is an ideology that presumes that the only knowledge and truth that matter are those that can be measured. Truth is understood as a collection of facts. In this view, knowledge and truth are falsely positioned as coming from nowhere and being delinked from particular subjective interests and ideologies that underlie truth claims. The current craze for measuring educational quality and progress through standardized testing nicely illustrates contemporary positivism. Standardized tests are comprised of questions that presume particular assumptions, values, and interests. Yet the student never gets to engage in dialogue with the actual people who develop the tests. Students never get to inquire as to the class and cultural background, values, and assumptions of the testmaker. The information and questions on the test are falsely presented as neutral, objective, and apolitical. Key questions are hidden such as, "Why is this on the test rather than that which is excluded?" "Whose knowledge and interests does this view represent?" "Whose perspectives and interests are framed out of the test and why?" "How does the selection of these particular truth claims relate to material interests or other broader social struggles and forces?" Additionally, positivist ideology denies the inevitably ethical dimensions of teaching.

The current drive for expanding a common core curriculum is a manifestation of this positivism and is thoroughly at odds with a conception of the cultural politics of knowledge. The common core idea suggests that it is a lack of homogeneity—that is, too much difference with regard to knowledge—that threatens the quality of schooling. If everyone could be tested on the same things, so goes the thinking, then we would be able to improve the quality of education because we would be able to more closely control its delivery. The common core project shares the same basic assumptions with the standardized testing craze. Knowledge ought to be measurable and deliverable, and there is a singular canon that everyone ought to know.

Unfortunately, by being tied to a goal of "preparing students for the workforce," common core designers have radically reduced literature and fiction to favor so-called informational texts such as heating insulations manuals. The common core represents a threat to schooling as a site that can foster imagination, interpretation, and judgment, which are required for capable citizenship to creatively address public problems. Moreover the common core renders schooling an adjunct to a particularly simple-minded notion of worker training.

In contrast, a central aim of the tradition of critical pedagogy, as characterized by the work of Henry Giroux, is to emphasize a view of knowledge, curriculum, and pedagogy in which cultural politics is central to teaching and learning. The value for cultural politics suggests that dialogue, debate, dissent, and habits of engaged curiosity become the lifeblood of schooling as they are the lifeblood of democracy. Teaching in this view is recognized as an inherently political endeavor, and teachers ought to be up front about the values and ideologies that they embrace. The struggle over culture from the critical view is always about the struggle for the formation of individual subjectivity that is pedagogically formed.

One of Giroux's concepts, **cultural pedagogy**, helpfully describes how cultural products and institutions educate people and hence require questioning for the pedagogical effects they have and the meanings and interests related to their production, circulation, and interpretation. Cultural pedagogy describes the struggle over culture, a struggle that is also about the formation of society and its institutions, public values, and public discourse from which individuals and groups draw their conceptual inventories. There are, in short, high social stakes in the ways that teachers make meanings and work to form culture. At the same time culture as meaning-making activity is dynamic and in play; it is always open to individual and collective creativity and imagination. Culture is constrained by historically inherited meanings and determining patterns, yet it is also on some level radically indeterminate and open to being remade. Hence, it would be a dire mistake to accept a cultural theory in which culture, knowledge, language, and curriculum are mere effects of a large force such as the economy, work, or history.

Suggested Further Reading

E. D. Hirsch. *Cultural Literacy: What Every American Needs to Know*. New York: Houghton Mifflin, 1987.

This is the key text of the common core view of culture as a body that needs to be canonized and then transmitted.

Donaldo Macedo. *Literacies of Power: What Americans Are Not Allowed to Know*. New York: Westview Press, 1994.

Macedo reconceptualizes the "cultural literacy" project to suggest a number of key concepts that animate a literacy of power. For Macedo, like Freire with whom he worked, literacy is inseparable from reading the world.

Henry Giroux. *Border Crossings: Cultural Workers and the Politics of Education*, 2nd ed. New York: Routledge, 2005.

Giroux updates critical pedagogy's engagement with culture to include critical multiculturalism, public pedagogy, and the cultures of security and militarism since September 11.

Stuart Hall. *Representation: Cultural Representations and Signifying Practices*, "Introduction," "Chapter One," and "Chapter Four." Thousand Oaks, CA: Sage, 1997.

Hall presents his constructivist theory of representation distinguishing it from reflective and intentional theories that tend to dominate popular thought. Hall brings together structuralist and poststructuralist thinkers to emphasize how culture is dynamic and based on exchanges of meanings, albeit always unequal ones. Giroux among others has drawn on Hall's theory of culture to expand on the role of teachers as meaning makers or cultural workers who are always "doing politics" when they act pedagogically.

Michael Apple. *Ideology and Curriculum*. New York: Routledge, 1979.

Apple draws on Antonio Gramsci, Raymond William, Pierre Bourdieu, and early Stuart Hall to explain the politics struggles over curriculum and connect education to broader social struggles.

Pierre Bourdieu. "The Forms of Capital." In *Handbook for Theory and Research for the Sociology of Education*, ed. J. Richardson, trans. Richard Nice, 46–58. New York: Greenwood, 1986.

Bourdieu explains how capital, social capital, and cultural capital allow for the reproduction of the class hierarchy and that these forms of capital are exchangeable.

Pierre Bourdieu and Jean-Claude Passeron. *Reproduction in Education, Society and Culture*. Thousand Oaks, CA: Sage, 1990 (orig. French edition 1970).

Bourdieu and Passeron explain how education is involved in the reproduction of the class structure. Their account highlights the ways that there is a symbolic economy of culture and differs from other versions of reproduction that see culture as a reflection of material relations of production.

Paulo Freire. *Pedagogy of the Oppressed*. New York: Continuum, 1970.

Freire, one of the founding figures of critical pedagogy, draws on Hegel, Marx, Sartre, Fromm, Cabral, and Fanon to put forward a pedagogy for humanistic liberation. Freire explains how oppression comes from dehumanization and that the aim of the humanizing pedagogy is to turn the experience of oppression into an object of critical analysis in order to work with others to transform reality and eliminate oppressive forces. Freire aims to help students not be treated as objects but to become subjects of history capable of acting on it and shaping it. This is one of the most important works of critical pedagogy.

Henry Giroux. *Theory and Resistance in Education*. Westport, CT: Bergin & Garvey, 1983.

Giroux engages with reproduction theory, the Frankfurt school of critical theory, and critical sociology of education to reconceptualize the possibilities for student and teacher agency. This text highlights the limitations of the reproduction theories of Althusser, Bourdieu, and Bowles and Gintis suggesting that critical pedagogy for the development of critical consciousness and social action ought not deny mediation, agency, and culture as a creative, not just structuring, force. This is one of the most important foundational works of critical pedagogy.

Theodor Adorno. *Introduction to Sociology*. Stanford, CA: Stanford University Press, 2000.

This lecture series offers a clear and compelling explanation of critical sociology and criticism of positivist ideology, which has been resurgent in the push to standardize curriculum and expand standardized testing.

Lilia Bartholome. "Beyond the Methods Fetish: Toward a Humanizing Pedagogy." *Harvard Education Review* 64 (Summer 1994): 190.

Bartholome provides a valuable criticism of the tendency in education to remove teaching methods from the broader social, political, and ethical concerns behind curriculum and pedagogy.

Questions for Discussion

1. How does the recognition of cultural politics differ from the conservative and liberal views of cultural transmission?
2. Why would teachers benefit from comprehending culture as struggled over rather than as transmitted?
3. How does positivist educational policy such as standardization and standardized testing deny cultural politics, and what are the social implications of such denials?
4. How would a robust sense of cultural politics in education contribute to a more expansive democratic society?

Chapter Two
The Political Economy of Education

This chapter begins by explaining what is meant by "political economy" and then examines how the ownership and control of schooling matters in terms of public interests and values, the cultural politics of the curriculum, and the reproduction of a class hierarchy. What is the difference between public and private control of schools and curriculum? How does the ownership and control of schools relate to economic formations and relationships throughout society? Can schooling be imagined as the basis for a more just egalitarian economic arrangement that democratizes economic relationships and undermines social hierarchies?

In the last two decades in the United States, the meaning and purpose of public education has been radically redefined. Across the political spectrum a consensus has emerged that defines the purpose of public schooling as primarily economic. Public schools are incessantly referred to in mass media and policy as being responsible for preparing the nation for global economic competition and preparing students to compete in the domestic economy. Following the economic crisis of 2008, everyone from the president of the United States to the chairman of the Federal Reserve Bank to *New York Times* columnist Thomas Friedman explained that the solution to the unemployment crisis required not creating jobs but reforming public schooling. And such reform more frequently than not called for treating public schools like private industry—injecting competition and choice, privatization and deregulation, into schooling.

The public school system has in fact since the early 1980s been subject to incessant declarations of "failure." Such judgments have been used to justify the expansion of market-based approaches to school management as well as to reimagine public schools as private businesses, educational leaders as CEOs, and students as customers. These policies involve a cultural project to frame public schooling as private, to portray society as a collection of atomistic consumers and workers. But these policies also involve an economic project of educating certain kinds of workers for the capitalist economy, setting the stage to capture the wealth of the public sphere for investors. These latter economic struggles over public schools are the focus of this chapter.

Political Economy and Social Reproduction in Schooling

Political economy is an expression that predates modern economics. While modern economics restricts its concerns to microeconomic and macroeconomic activity, largely delinking the economy from politics and culture, **political economy** offered a much broader theoretical framing of economics, asking questions about the relationships between economy and nature, culture, and politics. Political economy asks us to think about the economy in relation to the totality of social life rather than restricting economic concerns to questions such as supply, demand, money, and prices. Narrow economic framing of the relationship between education and the economy tends to treat students as future workers and consumers, focusing on producing the labor supply for industry and presenting individual economic possibilities through a promise of upward mobility. Within this view, more schooling offers greater access and inclusion into the existing economic arrangement.

In the 1970s and 1980s scholars from the critical perspective raised a number of crucial questions about the relationship between education and the economy. In the U.S. context, theorists of social and cultural reproduction such as **Samuel Bowles and Herbert Gintis** in *Schooling in Capitalist America* challenged the conventional wisdom that saw schooling as an equality-promoting device. They found that schooling largely functioned to deepen and entrench the racialized class order under the guise of merit. They empirically demonstrated that the determinant of students' future wealth and income is a student's class position and family wealth and income rather than either intelligence or amount of schooling.

Bowles and Gintis sought to explain how schools are centrally involved in making workers for capitalism. Particularly, they described how schools educate students not just with the job skills and knowledge useful for business owners but also for hierarchical social relationships conducive to future domination by a boss. They called this process the "correspondence principle," which had five key components:

1. Economic inequality in the society is mostly a function of markets and the broader economy not of the education system.
2. Schooling educates students to understand inequality as natural and deserved and to accept social hierarchy in forms that are useful for owners in the economy.
3. The reproduction of the economy is accomplished to a large extent by educating students into hierarchical relationships that correspond to the hierarchical relationships of the workplace.
4. Education is contradictory and complex with school producing not just docile and disciplined workers but also misfits and rebels.
5. The form of schooling corresponds to the particular historical moment of the economy and to popular struggles associated with efforts for capital accumulation.

For reproduction theorists, the capitalist economy can only continue to function if individuals learn to take their preordained place as worker or boss. School reproduces the class hierarchy while making it appear as if school rewards merit or talent rather than family wealth and income. That is, schools do not only teach skills and know-how; they teach skills and know-how thoroughly wrapped in class-based ideology.

Reproduction theorists from Europe, particularly **Louis Althusser** and **Pierre Bourdieu**, similarly contended that schooling largely serves to reproduce social relationships for capitalism. Bourdieu focused on how schools added to the **cultural capital** of privileged classes while punishing those students who don't already bring cultural capital with them. Althusser explained how the school functions as the principal **ideological state apparatus (ISA)**. As an ideological state apparatus, the school is the site where students are formed as ideological subjects or **interpellated**. That is, they are "called in" to the place that the state has already reserved for them, and only by answering this call do they become subjects. Though subjects were historically formed through the call of the church, the school has replaced the church as the principal site where subjects are called into relation with the plans of the state. Through the rituals and practices of the school, ideology most often succeeds: students come to recognize themselves as "good subjects" of those in positions of authority. For Althusser the making of particular kinds of subjects ultimately came back to the reproduction of the capitalist economy and social organization.

Reproduction theorists emphasized that the principal way for profit to be made in a capitalist economy is by exploiting workers: paying them less than their time and labor power is worth. The economy can only be continually re-created if workers learn to take their place and play their role in the production process. The reproduction theorists emphasize that the hierarchical arrangement of the capitalist economy is not necessarily the most efficient form of production, but it is the most efficient in terms of maintaining a hierarchical control over the production process. In order for a tiny portion of the population to retain control and ownership over industry, a highly antidemocratic form of relating to other people must be taught and learned.

Working-class and professional-class schools reproduce the stratified labor force while making such unequal sorting and sifting appear as a matter of either merit or natural talent. Schools in working-class communities are subject to punitive, rigid, disciplinary reforms that are designed to instill in students submission to hierarchical control. Scripted lessons, direct instruction, strict bodily codes demanding students' feet on floor and hands on desk and eyes on the teacher, uniforms, strict speaking codes, uniform lessons—these celebrated though not necessarily good school reforms targeting working-class and poor students aim to make docile, disciplined subjects who will submit to the authority of the teacher and later submit to the authority of the boss and ever worsening work conditions of low-skill, low-pay work in a deregulated globalizing economy.

Reproduction theorists emphasize that the ways we should understand class is in terms not simply of wealth and income (haves and have-nots or 1 percent/99 percent as the Occupy movement has popularized) but rather the question of the ownership and control of the production processes of the society, including ideological processes. What are people's relationship to owning and controlling industry? We can recognize at least four broad economic classes by their different relationship to ownership and control of production processes:

1. People in the ruling class own the production process.
2. People in the professional class manage the production process for the ruling class. Knowledge workers, including teachers, journalists, advertisers, and those with advanced specialized technical knowledge, are in this class.
3. People in the working class do most of the work of making these industries run but don't control or manage them.
4. "Throwaways" are those who are marginalized from the production process.

People might be distributed differently in these class categories according to other social categories like race, gender, ethnicity, nationality, age, ability, and so on. For example, an immigrant worker in domestic service getting paid off the books might merge class 3 with class 4, demonstrating that there are workers inside the production process whose wages and conditions of employment are kept low by being identified as "disposable."

Despite the tendency to see most of the United States as middle class, in fact the United States has a quite pronounced class hierarchy with the lowest upward class mobility among the industrialized nations. And classes have interests that are fundamentally antagonistic to other classes. For example, the ruling class has a necessary interest in expanding the profitability of their businesses in order to compete against other businesses. In order to continually expand profit, owners cut labor costs and benefits and security. These interests run contrary to those of workers who have an interest in higher wages and benefits and greater job security. The ultimate interest of workers would be in sharing in the ownership and control of the production process, ending the ruling class monopoly over the production process.

School plays an important role in mediating these class conflicts, including educating all students to understand their interests as aligned with rather than antagonistic to ruling class interests. Schools further the ruling class ideology that naturalizes the radically unequal social order as fair and just and most importantly a matter of individual merit and talent rather than a system that unequally distributes life chances. They also displace the class hierarchy onto cultural categories, positioning alleged cultural deficits as a cause of educational and hence economic inequality confusing and covering over the institutional maintenance of a racialized class hierarchy.

As Bertell Ollmann emphasizes, one way of maintaining this ideology is through a heavy emphasis on standardized testing. Such testing instills in students a number of implicit values designed to further the interests of the owners of businesses. The emphasis on student discipline and docility through the enforcement of standardized regimes reveals what Ollman calls the real lessons of testing: obeying authority, understanding truth to reside with those in power, and preparing for work speed-ups. Such discipline becomes crucial in the context of a steadily worsening economy in the United States as factories—and with them unionized and secure jobs—have been shipped overseas in the past few decades under the economic dictates of neoliberalism (see Chapter Seven).

Ollman also rightly suggests that business has discovered in public education a rich source of profit. As profit has become tougher to extract in the private sector, corporations and investors look to seize portions of the public sector, through lucrative contracts in for-profit school management and a vast array of educational products and services. The profit made by investors drains public resources that would otherwise be spent on educational services. The standardized testing push of the 2000s was interwoven with the financial interests of test makers and textbook publishers, curriculum producers, and contracting companies including technology firms. The standardization of knowledge through standardized testing and standardization of curriculum lends itself to the financial pursuits of fiscal conservatives or neoliberals who want to treat knowledge as an industrial commodity and use private sector methods for delivery. As Michael Apple explains, such standardization makes cultural conservative common core approaches to knowledge especially attractive to fiscal conservatives.

Schooling under Fordism and Post-Fordism

In the era of the industrial **Fordist** economy of the twentieth century, public schools played an economic role of not just preparing workers and ideologically forming them but also of creating a "reserve army of labor." As an economic strategy for capital and the ruling class, schooling in the industrial economy had the public absorb the training costs for business while flooding the labor market to keep labor costs cheap for owners.

The Fordist economy was defined by industrial production and the post–World War II boom in unionized factory jobs, a compact between capital and labor, and a social arrangement characterized by time-intensive forms of social control such as psychotherapy, rehabilitative incarceration, social work, and a growing safety net for the expanding middle class. Schools reproduced a two-tiered workforce and represented a long-term investment in knowledge and skills of future workers. The post-Fordist economy from the early 1970s on, in contrast, has been marked by the replacement of unionized industrial work with low-paying, low-skill, and de-unionized service work, the suppression of real wages, increasing consumer debt, an individualized sense of economic responsibility, and the whittling away of the safety net. With the departure of industrial production to nations with cheap labor, the shift to the post-industrial service economy, and the expansion of neoliberal ideology, public schools are seen by capitalists as playing a new role in contributing to the wealth of the owners of industry. Short-term profit can be made by treating students as commodities as public schools are subject to contracting and privatization. Working-class and poor schools in urban and rural areas are targeted for for-profit school management and special educational service remediation schemes, test contracting, and database tracking contracts. The charter school and "turnaround" movement is playing a central role in closing unionized public schools and opening de-unionized schools ready for contracting. The for-profit management companies cannot get a foot in the door in the well-funded public schools in rich suburbs that often spend three times the amount spent in urban districts. After all, why would a rich district spending $25,000 per pupil accept the model of a for-profit management company that spends about $7,000 per pupil? But that same $7,000 expenditure makes sense in an urban district that spends $7,800 per pupil. Urban school districts have a long legacy of shortchanging working-class and poor citizens when it comes to education. Consequently, oftentimes residents go along with or even support privatization proposals, accepting the logic that the public system has failed. Of course, the public system has worked spectacularly well in the places where it has received both heavy funding and political commitment to its success.

Since the 1990s, experiments with market-based approaches to school reform have turned into the dominant approach, with privatized management in the form of **charter schools, school vouchers**, and **scholarship tax credits**. Large private **educational management organizations** are increasingly merging into large businesses, and the charter school movement continues to expand the role of for-profit companies in running public schools.

Why does it matter who owns and controls public schools? There are several reasons why it matters who owns and controls public schools. Part of what makes public schools "public" is the fact that they are owned and controlled by many people rather than narrowly owned and controlled by one or just a few. Converting that public ownership to private ownership and control affects finances, curriculum and pedagogy, school culture and administration, secrecy, transparency and accountability, and even identity. When a public school is privately managed, public oversight and governance is shifted to private parties, financial accountability can be made secret, and the curriculum and subject matter will tend to be largely constrained to the ideologies and institutional interests of those private businesses running schools. As education industries increasingly converge with for-profit security companies, test and textbook publishing, and database tracking industries, the public interest, community values, and emancipatory values become subjugated to the pursuit of financial profits.

Perhaps most important, there are dire implications for schools becoming places where students learn to think only in terms of the private interests of those running schools for profit rather than in the public interests of the community, the nation, and the world. In other words, schools are a place where students develop as selves. A society of purely private selves is very different from a society of people who share a sense of public and civic values as well.

Limitations of Economic Perspectives: Human Agency and Resistance

In the late 1970s and early 1980s, critical scholars such as Henry Giroux and Stanley Aronowitz emphasized the theoretical limitations of social and cultural reproduction, including the fact that these theories so emphasize domination that the **agency** of teachers and students appears weak at best. Giroux and Aronowitz also emphasized the extent to which reproduction theory was caught in a long history of Marxian **economism** that mistakenly presumes class and economy to be the foundational and most important concern for questions of freedom and justice, that defines human beings through the metaphor of production, and that is wrapped up in a legacy that includes patriarchy, technological mastery, and the exploitation of nature. As Giroux and Aronowitz argue, culture has primacy over economics in forming society. Material, resources, and money only become meaningful or intelligible through culture, language, and values. For example, greed, an understanding of the self through commodity acquisition, or to the contrary collectivism, and an understanding of the self through giving, are not natural positions but learned values that only make sense in a cultural context. Despite its limitations, social and cultural reproduction theory continues to be particularly useful in accounting for current educational reform proposals that are in vogue in the United States, and it remains a valuable theoretical tool for making sense of the incessantly repeated claims about the uses of schooling for the capitalist economy.

As previously mentioned, working-class students are subject to pedagogies of control and repression oriented around either making them docile and disciplined workers for the low-pay, low-skill bottom end of the economy or warehousing them for a future of social and economic marginalization and disposability—the school-to-prison pipeline exemplifying this path. For professional-class students the pedagogies are radically different: dialogue and speaking out are encouraged as students are assumed to be thinking agents who are being groomed to exercise control in the private sector and in government. These different schools for different classes teach more than just different skills and know-how. As Henry Giroux notes, they also teach different senses of **agency**—the sense of their capacity to act on the world they inhabit. Giroux emphasizes that democratic societies require not only educated citizens but critical citizens who are armed with the tools of interpretation and the sense of agency to challenge individual and collective injustices and in the best tradition of democracy to collectively control life conditions.

Suggested Further Reading

Samuel Bowles and Herbert Gintis. *Schooling in Capitalist America*. Chicago: Haymarket Books, 2011 (orig. 1976).

In the U.S. context this is the foundational text elaborating on how the school reproduces the class hierarchy. This book was out of print for decades despite being heavily cited in critical literature.

Pierre Bourdieu. "The Forms of Capital." In *Handbook for Theory and Research for the Sociology of Education*, ed. J. Richardson, trans. Richard Nice, 46–58. New York: Greenwood, 1986.

Bourdieu explains how capital, social capital, and cultural capital allow for the reproduction of the class hierarchy and that these forms of capital are exchangeable.

Louis Althusser. "Ideology and Ideological State Apparatuses (Notes towards an Investigation)." In *Mapping Ideology*, ed. Slavoj Zizek, 100–140. New York: Verso, 1994 (orig. 1970).

Althusser's ISA essay elaborates on how reproduction of the capitalist economy requires ideological subject formation, which is done in the ideological state apparatuses such as schools, media, and other knowledge-making institutions. Althusser explains how ISAs make consent to domination while the repressive state apparatuses (RSAs) work through coercion to enforce the state's rules, which operate on behalf of capital. Althusser emphasizes that ideology, which works by interpellating or hailing subjects, is material being enacted by rituals and practices and that it is also imaginary, representing the subjects' imaginary relationship to the relations of production in the economy. Giroux's *Theory and Resistance* offers a valuable discussion of insights and limitations of Althusser's position.

Kenneth Saltman. *The Failure of Corporate School Reform.* Boulder, CO: Paradigm, 2012.

Saltman upends contemporary claims that public schooling has failed, arguing instead that the neoliberal restructuring of privatization, deregulation, and the applications of corporate culture to schooling fail to not just raise test scores and cut costs but also fail the public purposes of public schooling. Saltman suggests that reproduction theory be selectively revived and that it now accounts for the ways that a new two-tiered education system is being created that commodifies and privatizes public schools and students who have been subject to historical disinvestment and who are rendered redundant to the reproduction of capital outside of schools. Saltman calls for the creation of a new common school movement to imagine public schools forging collective labor and learning for collective control over property and work.

Michael Apple. *Educating the Right Way.* New York: Routledge, 2001.

Apple maps the variety of rightist movements: neoliberal, neoconservative, religious right, and authoritarian populist as they appear in education.

Henry A. Giroux. *Theory and Resistance in Education.* Westport, CT: Bergin & Garvey, 1983.

Giroux offers a valuable criticism to the theoretical limitations of reproduction theory and initiates a revalued emphasis on the importance of culture for critical education.

Stanley Aronowitz and Henry Giroux. *Education Still Under Siege.* Westport, CT: Bergin & Garvey, 1989.

Paul Willis. *Learning to Labor: How Working Class Kids Get Working Class Jobs.* New York: Columbia University Press, 1977.

Willis's ethnographic study of British youth was very influential on attempts to theorize student opposition and resistance.

Nadine Dolby and Greg Demitriadis. *Learning to Labor in New Times.* New York: Routledge, 2004.

Dolby and Demitriadis revisit Willis's key concerns.

Bertell Ollman. "Why So Many Exams? A Marxist Response." *Z Magazine*, October 2002. http://www.nyu.edu/projects/ollman/docs/why_exams.php.

Ollman's short article was prescient in explaining how the expansion of privatization and standardized testing relates to neoliberal globalization.

Richard Wolff. *Capitalism Hits the Fan*. Film. http://www.capitalismhitsthefan.com/.

Wolff's film offers a concise and brilliant explanation for the 2008 financial crisis, putting it in the context of 150 years of U.S. economics. The film shows how wage repression in the 1970s resulted in massive debt expansion to maintain consumer spending. The result was vast corporate and bank profits but the creation of a massive bubble economy. Wolff argues that the fundamental solution is to end the separation of workers from managers and to opt for a democratic economy.

Questions for Discussion

1. What are the dominant assumptions about the relationship between education and the economy?
2. In what ways does reproduction theory differ from the dominant explanations of the relationship between education and the economy?
3. Why does it matter who owns and controls education?
4. What are the implications of understanding economic class as it is described in the chapter as opposed to in terms of haves and have-nots or the 1 percent and the 99 percent?
5. If democracy is concerned with freedom and equality, how do these democratic values relate to the different conceptions of education and the economy?
6. What are the limitations of reproduction theory?
7. Why might reproduction continue to be important despite its limitations?

Chapter Three
The Political Psychology of Education

Drawing predominantly on Erich Fromm, Paulo Freire, Michel Foucault, Slavoj Zizek, and feminist education scholars informed by psychoanalysis, this chapter considers ego psychology and poststructuralist psychology as alternatives to the dominant psychological stains of educational psychology and human development. The chapter uses the critical psychology approaches to problematize depoliticized versions of educational psychology and highlights the assets and limitations of humanist and poststructuralist critical perspectives for considering policy and practice. The discussion distinguishes character education from the pedagogical making of what Fromm calls social character and challenges psychological theories that deny the possibility for the pedagogical formation of critical consciousness.

A Critical Psychology of Education

Dominant strains of educational psychology and human development suggest that teaching and learning require a neutral and universally applicable psychological science. In this view, if we know, for example, how the brain develops or what the normal stages of behavioral development corresponding to age are, then we know what, how, and when to teach. In contrast to the dominant psychological perspectives, critical psychologies emphasize that individual psychology is socially and historically produced, infused with power relations, and struggled over politically. The self, in the critical view, is not understood as an essential entity that can be understood as biologically determined, pre-social, or natural. Rather the self is socially, culturally, linguistically, and historically constituted, is not essential and biologically determined, and is subject to the historical play of power struggles by competing material interests and symbolic positions of classes, racial, ethnic, gender, and sex groups. The critical view does not deny biology and nature but recognizes that the biological and natural realities of a person only become meaningful culturally. While there are numerous critical theories of psychology, in what follows here I focus briefly and principally on the psychology of education found in Paulo Freire's foundational scholarship on critical pedagogy and the psychoanalytic critical theory of Erich Fromm, whom Freire relies upon in his work. Then I turn to the emphases placed on critical psychology by feminist education scholars.

Critical psychological theories share a belief that identity is always in formation, that the formation of identity cannot be understood apart from the social forces and struggles informing its development, and that the self should not be understood as being a mere effect of natural biology. The self, in short, is the object of social and political struggles. At the same time critical psychological theories emphasize the importance of the self developing **autonomy** and **agency**—that is, the capacity to act on and shape collectively the material world that individuals inhabit. The self is not only the object of social and political struggles in this view but also a subject endowed with different capacities to shape the social world. The subject and the world are co-terminous: each develops and evolves within the other, meaning that neither one precedes the other or is an effect of the other. For proponents of critical pedagogy such as Paulo Freire and Henry Giroux, a crucial question is, *how are subjects produced pedagogically*? Critical pedagogists advocate for educative forces that foster critical interpretations and that lead to acts of social intervention toward the end of human emancipation from domination and oppression and toward the end of democratic social relations. The tradition of critical pedagogy rejects a deterministic view of the self that sees it as an effect of the social world and also rejects a voluntaristic view of the self that sees it as individually shaping its own world and life possibilities. We are in fact miseducated on a regular basis into seeing ourselves and others as passive objects incapable of intervening in social realities. For example, such commonplace practices as television punditry and sports spectatorship are effective ways of educating individuals into passive and spectatorial ways of seeing. Politics becomes a game for elites and we are authorized to be commenting on the sidelines. We are also miseducated regularly into seeing ourselves as "super-agents" solely responsible for our situations and life chances. Testing in schools and popular culture such as action movies or comic books or advertisements effectively teaches us that we ought to accept that our lack of power or material wealth or control over our life conditions is due to our own individual failure to live up to an impossible superhuman standard as opposed to a system that is designed by and run for the benefit of a few at the top of the economic and political systems.

From the perspective of critical pedagogy, the pedagogical formation of the self is inextricably intertwined with broader political struggles and with ethical responsibility. Self-formation happens not only in formal schooling environments such as schools but throughout a culture. All meaning-making activities that individuals do have pedagogical aspects. So psychological interventions in critical educational practice are concerned with not merely therapeutic investigation of individual experience toward, for example, a cathartic unburdening of the contents of inner life. Individual experience is rather interpreted and theorized through social theoretical analysis that elucidates how subjective experience is produced through the play of social forces.

Theorizing inner experience becomes the basis for reconstructing it in relation to public problems animating it. Paulo Freire famously taught Brazilian peasants to read the word by reading the world. But this investigation began with what those peasants experienced. The peasants had been miseducated to understand their hunger through dominant ideological tropes such as the will of god, fatalism, and so on. Freire problematized this experience in terms of the structural forces of capitalism and their specific manifestations in that context, including the exploitation by agrarian landholders. The project of critical pedagogy is one of humanization: to struggle to be an active subject rather than to be treated as an object for the exploitation of others. Freire draws on Fromm's critical psychoanalysis to explain that the oppressors who seek to dehumanize, exploit, and objectify others are in a sadomasochistic relationship with the oppressed. The oppressors "inanimate" the oppressed, seeking to make the oppressed into dead things that can be controlled. The **banking education** practices that Freire excoriates are a pedagogical practice that treats the oppressed as empty vessels to be filled (as objects) with objectified knowledge treated as units of commodity or cash.

Freedom for the oppressors is learned as the freedom to oppress others and not to be oppressed by others. The burden of revolutionary pedagogy for Freire is for the oppressed to not simply invert the oppressor-oppressed relation and themselves to become the new oppressors. Rather, the oppressed bear a double burden of freeing themselves and freeing the oppressors. A psychological challenge for critical pedagogy is to deal with the **adhesion** that the oppressed experience. The oppressed learn from the earliest age that to be free is to be the oppressor. So a critical pedagogy must challenge the identification that the oppressed have with the oppressor. A crucial task for any critical pedagogy is the making of new forms of identification with which to identify, forms of identification that are founded in relations of equality and democracy and that defy the objectification and instrumentalizaton of individuals.

For Freire, critical pedagogy aims toward the vocation of becoming more fully human. That is, the aim is to be a **subject** of history rather than to be an **object**—to act on the world rather than to be simply acted upon. To put it differently, Freire imagines a society of politically empowered social actors rather than a society of passive spectators. People must act by being in the world. Freire insists that inevitably one takes political positions whether one is aware of those positions or whether one simply gives in to hopelessness and resignation about the world as it is. Freire's perspective draws stark lines between the subject categories of oppressor and oppressed.

Despite Freire's classification of people into the categories of oppressor or oppressed, in teaching Freire in the United States I have found that most students see themselves as both oppressors (in a position to dehumanize and objectify others) and as oppressed (being dehumanized and objectified by others). These students are variously dehumanized and objectified as workers, treated as instruments for the profit accumulation of owners of businesses; as teachers who are expected to treat students as objectified receptacles for objectified knowledge; and as women who are objectified by sexist advertisements. Teaching Freire with teacher candidates in the United States also highlights the extent to which subjectivity and student experience is overwhelmingly formed through identifications with mass media representations.

Henry Giroux has probably done more than anyone in extending Freire's thinking into considerations of media representations. Such media representations function pedagogically and politically offering subject positions, points of identification, values, and ideological constellations with which individuals locate themselves. As Giroux explains, this is why students need to develop their capacities to criticize and interpret media and other representations in terms of the ethical, political, and social values they promote. Yet interpretation ought to form the basis for collective action to transform the social forces producing representations and also as the basis for students to become cultural producers themselves.

The Specificity of Context and Student Experience

Most contemporary educational reforms tend toward standardizing knowledge and curriculum. For example, the expansion of a common core curriculum standard and the expansion of standardized testing have resulted in the de-emphasis on individual student experience other than as a potential obstacle or deficit to the reproduction of **official knowledge**. Critical education—particularly in the work of Freire, Dewey, and Giroux—emphasizes that pedagogy ought to be meaningful to be made critical, to be socially transformative. That means that experience and the local context are analyzed in relation to broader economic, political, and cultural forces that produce the experience and context. Such analysis of experience and context become the basis for transforming the students' understanding of what they experience as oppressive, objectifying, and dehumanizing, such that they can learn to act collectively to challenge and transform the forces that make the experience. Too often experience in education is treated as if it is the final arbiter of truth. It is common for working teachers to denigrate educational theory and scholarship on the basis that teachers are "in the trenches" and hence their experience speaks for itself. In fact, experience needs to be theorized and problem-posed in relation to broader social forces that make it and in terms of the cultural values and assumptions that make experience intelligible in particular ways.

Society and Selves Constituted by Difference

Critical social theories and critical perspectives on psychology share an assumption that the self and the society are constituted by difference, change, and contestation. The assumption spans the Freudian and Marxian traditions and has been carried forward in numerous theories ranging from **critical theory**, **radical democracy**, and **poststructuralism**. Critical social theory presumes that society is constituted by difference in the form of social antagonisms between competing groups (this is taken up through the idea of Gramsci's hegemony, which I discuss in Chapter Four). For example, ruling-class people who own production processes have interests and corresponding ideologies that are at odds with the interests of working-class people. In order for owners to compete in industries, they need to maximize profits and cut costs by reducing pay and benefits for workers. In order to have a rising material standard of living, workers need demand increases in pay and benefits. These groups have material interests that are at odds. Yet dominant liberal and neoliberal **discourse** educates everybody with the falsehood that everybody can have shared interests and that if individuals work hard and follow the rules of the game everyone can benefit.

This denial of class antagonism is particularly pronounced in education through the official discourse of inclusion, access, and meritocracy. Every student is taught that everyone can learn knowledge that is deemed to be universally valuable. Failure to learn this knowledge becomes the basis for justifying educational and then social and economic exclusion as the fault of the individual. In this example, we see how the self is formed through social antagonism. Few individuals escape having their desires, values, and ideologies at least in part shaped by the pedagogies found in educative institutions including schools, the family, mass media, religion, and the legal system. Most children learn dominant values through compulsory schooling and accept these as natural, normal, and inevitable. Such values include the normalcy of competition for scarce resources, punctuality, quantifiable progress, submission to the decisions of those in positions of authority, the fundamental beneficence or legitimacy of the government, the boss, and of a capitalist economy, and the measure of the self by its power to consume.

These dominant values are often contradictory, and often values within these educative institutions contradict each other. For example, early childhood education and religion both emphasize sharing, giving, and care for others, countering the emphasis on competition and exclusionary forms of schoolwork ("eyes on your own paper!"). Individuals internalize these contradictory values. Regular educational promotion demands that the student give the teacher "goodwill" and that obedience in accordance with the dominant social values become deeply internalized. While dominant ideologies are successfully installed in subjects through the pedagogical work of institutions and individuals, these ideologies and the identifications that subjects make of representations are struggled over and hardly guaranteed. Subcultural **resistance** thrives and can form the basis for organized resistance and **counterhegemonic** cultural forms in which people collectively develop emancipatory projects and movements.

Constitutive antagonism in the society and the self involves culture as well, and, in fact, culture may be more determining of material realities. Different cultural-linguistic and ethnic groups compete for cultural dominance, as discussed in Chapter Four.

Repression

In the late nineteenth century, the logic of repression became pronounced in the social sciences and humanities. "Repression" happens when someone has an experience that is too painful or traumatic to accept or that falls outside of his or her established conceptual framework; the individual is able to repress this experience, forget it, erase it (but, according to psychoanalysis, only partially!). Friedrich Nietzsche wrote in *The Twilight of the Idols* about how the history of the West has involved the repression of difference and darkness, favoring, instead, positivity and light. Nietzsche saw the denial of negativity as a kind of sickness setting the stage for a culture to be haunted by those repressed realities. The Freudian and Marxian traditions both emphasize the centrality of different kinds of repression and the ways that there is a **return of the repressed**. Freud discovered or at least popularized the psychological unconscious. For the Freudian tradition repression was a necessity in order to sublimate or hold back violent and sexual drives that would, if acted out, threaten the social order. Repression for Freud was the price of civilization.

Some, most notably the Marxist philosopher Herbert Marcuse, recast Freudian repression in the 1960s. Marcuse suggested that in the social and economic conditions of advanced industrial capitalism, individuals and society suffered from excessive repression. Marcuse emphasized the liberation of libidinal (sexual and sensual) desire and saw this unleashing as potentially anchoring a radical reevaluation of the society and the development of a radically egalitarian politics that could counter the unfreedoms that characterize contemporary society like police repression, submission to drudgery in the workplace, and so on.

More recently, Slavoj Zizek has challenged Marcuse's ideas, suggesting that the emphasis on freeing desire in the 1960s and 1970s coincided with the radical expansion of consumerism. The focus on freeing desire may be just what contemporary consumer capitalism needs but is not necessarily compatible with emancipated subjects, according to Zizek. Zizek draws on French psychoanalyst Jacques Lacan in order to elaborate a theory of ideological self-formation. For Zizek, culture represses the Real, giving birth to a whole imaginary apparatus of imagery and narratives that serve to hide those moments when the Real could emerge. The Real refers to the traumatic kernel of reality that is only fleetingly apparent when ideology breaks down.

For Zizek, in the course of daily life, individuals actively engage in disavowal of the **Real**. An example: a teacher candidate student of mine told me that at her home she plays a looped recording of the science fiction/ horror film *Alien* on the television, including the times she spends preparing for class by reading critical pedagogy and the political economy of education. I was astonished to hear that she so immerses herself in this film (one of my favorites) that is about space travelers encountering and accidentally unleashing killer aliens who gestate in human hosts only to explode from their chests upon maturation. Though containing a fantastical premise, the film has a socially critical dimension to it, showing the corporation willing to sacrifice its employees in order to weaponize these acid-salivating killer alien creatures. Yet, in one class session in my course the same student walked out of a screening of John Pilger's documentary film *The War on Democracy* at the point in which an American nun sat in a chair and calmly recounted her torture and sexual assault at the hands of American-led paramilitaries in a Guatemalan prison. Pilger's film details the grotesque acts of violence that the United States has committed against civilians in Latin America and around the world in the name of national security interests—that is, to further the economic and strategic interests of rich investors and major corporations. Zizek's use of the Lacanian Real is valuable in this example because it highlights how, for example, the Pilger film approaches the traumatic reality of how things are really run by the American empire, the horrors being concealed by rhetoric of democracy, rights, and freedom. The student could saturate herself at home daily in the vivid imagery of disembowelment, burns, and beheadings in the form of science fiction but the recounting of the actual experience of torture told by a victim in a documentary was too close to the traumatic kernel of the Real in the self.

In fact, this example suggests that the constant screening of horror and terror as fiction may have done important ideological work for the student, emphatically emphasizing that these hidden terrors are fictions, contributing to the active repression of the traumatic Real, which Pilger's film details and brings to light. Zizek's insight is important because it speaks to the active **disavowal** at play in contemporary ideology: the "I know very well that ... but I do it anyway." We know that we are bringing humanity and other species to the point of extinction through the use of fossil fuels, but we burn them anyway. We know that politicians are spouting empty slogans and that contemporary democracy is a corporately managed democracy that approximates what Sheldon Wolin called **inverted totalitarianism**, but we play along. We know that the standards, testing, and privatization schemes are not about excellence but about a ritualized performance of control, but we play along.

A crucial task of critical pedagogy must be to cut through these ideologies. It is not enough to intervene in the pedagogical production of subjectivity by doing ideology critique and making ideology critique the basis for collective social transformation. It is necessary as well to confront the structure of disavowal in the various guises that it takes, such as the pedagogical production of the culture of cynicism that educates people to feel that public problems are inevitable and beyond political response and even to embrace political apathy as cool, chic, and admirable.

Zizek is hardly the only social theorist to draw on Jacques Lacan. A number of feminist psychoanalysts in education have used Lacan, most notably Sharon Todd, Deborah Britzman, Charles Bingham, and Elizabeth Ellsworth. Much of this work builds on Lacan's famous dictum that the unconscious is structured like a language. Lacan's conception of the self was indebted to Sausurrian structural linguistics, where signifiers (or meaning-units such as words or images) get their identities or significance through their difference with other signifiers, rather than through reference to a concept (an image already conceptualized in the brain: a signified) or to a thing in the world. This means that signifiers are uprooted, they play against each other rather than remaining fixed, tied to an object (we saw another interpretation of structural linguistics in Stuart Hall's term "signifying practices" in Chapter One). Feminist pedagogues have taken Lacan's appropriation of structural linguistics to mean that communication is impossible. For Ellsworth and her like, a teacher can have a lesson that she presents to her students, but the students receive something different, because words and meanings cannot be stabilized. Feminist pedagogues generally see this configuration as always true (no meanings are fixed or framed), and as a result, teaching—as an exercise in Reason—is impossible; irrationality is always inserting itself through language. Nevertheless, such self-labeled feminist pedagogues understand this practice of teaching and its impossible result as liberating, because the student ends up out of reach of the teacher's authority and so of all authority. Because it is structured like a language, the unconscious is, quite essentially, resistant, and it automatically escapes from any given knowledge.

Critical pedagogues would disagree with this argument on several counts. For one, they would not claim that the impossibility of teaching is radical, feminist, or emancipatory. As well, they would not assert that all authority is bad, deadening, or repressive, but would make a distinction between the inevitable pedagogical authority of the teacher, on the one hand, and, on the other, authoritarianism, the misuse of power. Third, critical pedagogy would not universalize the teacher-student relationship by saying that it is always framed through unjust power that is always undermined by the natural structure of language on which it relies. Critical pedagogy would not insist that power had to be privatized, in personal relations, but would rather reveal how power is a historical and social relationship formed by institutions and distributions of material goods and political positions. As Robin Truth Goodman explains, Ellworth, as well as her self-labeled feminist pedagogue associates,

> never questions or criticizes the collapse of feminism into a private interior identity based in desire, nor the politics of ignorance where anti-intellectualism can be elevated to a moral principle.... Ellsworth does not raise the issue of what this privatization has meant historically as it reduces the politics of femininity to the affiliative, the aesthetic, and the affective.... [She] disregards how the attribution of ignorance [or irrationality] has been wielded for marginalizing populations, closing schools, [and] shutting down opportunities. (*World, Class, Women*: 43–44)

Unlike the self-labeled feminist pedagogues, critical pedagogues would not argue against feminist politics and feminist traditions that all violence can be reduced to symbolic violence, or the violence of language.

The Productivity of Power in the Making of the Self

Psychoanalysis has been adulterated in popular culture and the self-help traditions to presume that by bringing the unconscious to the conscious mind, the person could be cured of physical or mental illness. While psychoanalysis has largely waned as a psychological treatment in the United States, the logic of psychological repression and the need for talking cures is deeply entrenched in the culture. Television shows like reality TV, talk shows, and investigative journalism shows, to name a few, are organized around the premise that the speaking subject will be freed by confessing the truth of their inner self to the viewer. French philosopher Michel Foucault radically problematized this popular conception of the repressed authentic self.

Michel Foucault challenged what he called the repressive hypothesis in psychoanalysis by showing how the talking cure was not merely a matter of unburdening the inner contents of the self but of inducing individuals to make themselves through speaking. In other words, Foucault suggested that the truth of the self is made through the acts of speaking or confessing. He described, for example, in *The History of Sexuality, Volume I,* the **confessional technology** that can be found in the confession of the Catholic church and on the psychotherapy couch. The confessional technology is more recently deployed on reality TV. In these places the participant in confession enters into a relationship with the listener. The listener is not simply the recipient of the alleged inner contents of the self but is also invested with power. As the confessor speaks the "truth" of him or herself, he or she also produces oneself as a subject.

Moreover, the confessor enters into a power relation with the one who receives the confession. In other words, to be a subject is also to be subject to the authority of others and institutions in which one does one's meaning-making practices. For example, we have all learned that the Victorians were particularly adept at repressing their sexuality. But, says Foucault, the repressive apparatus did nothing but talk about sex constantly, incessantly, and seamlessly across institutions. In developing the various mechanisms to be used to stop children from masturbating, for example, the church, the school, the army, the medical establishment, and the institutions of psychological scholarship all collaborated in *producing* the various identities that the masturbating child might become, thereby making various forms of sexuality imaginable; perversions became visible.

In the case of reality TV shows and confessional talk shows, the television viewer is not the confessor but rather the one receiving confession. Nonetheless, for Foucault **discourse** (he uses this term for signifying practices, speech acts, and representations in order to foreground the role of institutions and institutional language) produces particular **subject positions** for the listener or viewer to occupy. Foucault's perspective breaks with the Marxian tradition of thinking of subjects as being ideologically produced in ways that correspond ultimately and always to class and economic determinations. Foucault replaces the term "ideology" with "discourse" to emphasize truth as being an effect of power and knowledge. This view suggests that there is no getting outside of historically constituted power relations. This, however, does not mean that individuals are simply an effect of social forces. Individuals are both constituted by discourse and produce discourse by doing signifying practices.

What all this means for teachers is that they are, on the one hand, historically constituted discursive subjects who need to do the work of analyzing how they are produced as particular subjects. They are the result of politics and power relations, and to understand oneself and what one is doing politically and pedagogically require self-knowledge and ongoing self-analysis. On the other hand, teachers need to realize that their signifying practices in the classroom matter politically, as teachers are inevitably actively producing, reworking, affirming, or contesting already existing broader public discourses. Students are formed as subjects by entering into subject positions that teachers might be making.

Suggested Further Reading

Paulo Freire. *Pedagogy of the Oppressed*. New York: Continuum, 1970.

Freire advocates for a critical pedagogy focused on becoming more fully human and on students who are actors and agents in their world. Such a pedagogy also breaks down the ideology that those who are free are oppressors and those who oppress are free.

Erich Fromm. *Escape from Freedom*. New York: Holt, 1941.

Fromm's *Escape from Freedom* was widely read when it was published and is a founding work of social psychology. It brings together a social constructionist interpretation of Freud with a humanist version of Marx. Fromm explains how people enter into patterns of behavior in which they abdicate freedom through relations of masochism and sadism. He holds faith in the capacity of people to cut through the "chains of illusion," overcome alienation, and work to address the most pressing problems facing humanity such as war and nuclear annihilation.

Cornelius Castoriadis. *World in Fragments*. Stanford, CA: Stanford University Press 1997.

Castoriadis brings together psychoanalysis with left politics to argue for individual and collective autonomy. He focuses heavily on imagination.

His work has influenced critical educators and other critical sociologists including Henry Giroux and Zygmunt Bauman.

Henry Giroux. *Disturbing Pleasures.* New York: Routledge, 1992.

This remains an important transitional work in which Giroux began to focus on cultural politics of mass media and art and the pedagogy of cultural studies.

Herbert Marcuse. *Eros and Civilization.* Boston: Beacon Press, 1955.

In addition to Fromm and Adorno, Herbert Marcuse was a member of the Frankfurt School of Critical Theory who expanded on psychoanalysis. Marcuse reworked Freud's claim that repression is the price of civilization. He historicized it and suggested that a surplus of repression was destructive and imagined nonrepressive and libidinal social relations. Marcuse criticisms of oppressive power and the ways these are lived, and his hopefulness for freedom resonated powerfully with the social movements of the 1960s.

Chantal Mouffe. *The Return of the Political.* New York: Verso, 1992.

Belgian political philosopher Mouffe developed her radical democracy theory with Argentinian political philosopher Ernesto Laclau. They bring together Derridaean deconstruction, Rortyan pragmatism, to reimagine politics as constituted by difference. This is a political theory consistent with the poststructural linguistic turn of the 1980s and 1990s. Radical democracy presumes that the social and the individual are constituted by difference.

Theodor Adorno. *Introduction to Sociology.* Stanford, CA: Stanford University Press, 2000.

Adorno's lecture course offers a valuable introduction to critical sociology and refutes the ideology of positivism, which separates facts from their underlying values and assumptions. It offers a clear and crucial explanation of the relationship between subjectivity and objectivity, theory and practice.

Theodor Adorno and Max Horkheimer. *Dialectic of Enlightenment.* Stanford, CA: Stanford University Press, 2002 (orig. 1944).

The authors, drawing from Nietzsche and prefiguring later poststructuralists, highlight the ways in which the legacy of Enlightenment thought—in its relentless pursuit of progress, rationality, harmony, totality, and positivity—deny and repress difference and negativity, which resurge in the form of irrationalism and destruction. Today's obsessive observance of standardized testing (alleged to be more efficient since numerically quantifiable and measurable) contributes to the exacerbation of irrationality, anti-intellectualism, and evasion of public action to genuinely improve public schools.

Slavoj Zizek. *Welcome to the Desert of the Real.* New York: Verso, 2001.

Zizek, a leading figure in cultural studies and critical theory, draws on French psychoanalyst Jacques Lacan. He discusses contemporary disavowal and political cynicism.

Deborah Britzman. *Lost Subjects, Contested Objects.* Albany: SUNY Press, 1989.

Britzman is a leading feminist educational theorist who has drawn on and developed psychoanalysis.

Elizabeth Ellsworth. *Teaching Positions.* New York: Teachers College Press, 1998.

Ellsworth's feminist pedagogy draws on Lacan's appropriation of structural linguistics to mean that communication is impossible. For Ellsworth, the lesson that a teacher presents is always different from the lesson the students receive because words and meanings cannot be stabilized. For Ellsworth, this fact is liberating because it frees students from the authority of the teacher and hence all authority.

Sharon Todd (ed.). *Learning Desire: Perspectives on Pedagogy, Culture, and the Unsaid.* New York: Routledge, 1997.

Educational philosopher whose work has developed the relationship between education and psychoanalysis. More recently she has worked on the ethical thought of Emanuel Levinas.

Robin Truth Goodman. *World Class Women.* New York: Routledge, 2004.

Goodman's book critically engages with feminist pedagogy suggesting that it generally fails to address the crucial distinction between public and private spheres in the context of neoliberalism. Goodman draws on the legacy of critical pedagogy to address this.

Sheldon Wolin. *Democracy Incorporated: Managed Democracy and the Spectre of Inverted Totalitarianism.* Princeton, NJ: Princeton University Press, 2008.

Woldin asserts that the contemporary United States is characterized by an authoritarianism that differs from traditional state/fascist control. Instead, this "inverted totalitarianism" is a system of corporate domination of the state, the production of political apathy among the population, and the fiction of "managed democracy" in which money dominates political institutions and politics becomes a performance.

Michel Foucault. *The History of Sexuality, Vol. I.* New York: Vintage, 1977.

Foucault suggests that the truth of the self is made through the acts of speaking or confessing. He uses the term "discourse" to mean the signifying practices, speech acts, and representations that produces particular subject positions for the listener or viewer to occupy. Foucault's perspective breaks with the Marxian tradition of thinking of subjects as being ideologically produced in ways that correspond ultimately and always to class and economic determinations. Individuals are not simply an effect of social forces; they are both constituted by discourse and produce discourse by doing signifying practices.

Questions for Discussion

1. What are some of the ways that the self is formed socially, politically, and culturally rather than being merely a function of biological nature?
2. What does critical pedagogy emphasize about the self?
3. How is the view of the self as determined by repression different from Foucault's version of the self as producing itself through discourse?

CHAPTER FOUR
HEGEMONY

This chapter elaborates Antonio Gramsci's theory of hegemony as a theory of political struggle that makes culture, language, and education central. Gramsci's theory of hegemonic social change is particularly important for teachers for a number of reasons. First, he conceived of education as inherently political. Second, he conceived of politics as being educational. Third, he offered an elaborate theory of the role that education plays in making different kinds of political agency. Fourth, he emphasized the role of intellectuals (such as teachers) and by redefining the term "hegemony" through intellectual labor suggested important implications for educators. Fifth, he emphasized that ideas come not from the head alone but are the result of historical struggles.

Gramsci and Hegemony

Hegemony has two distinct meanings for social and political theorists. Hegemony can refer to dominant power. This is the more common meaning. Hegemony can also refer to struggle between different groups for social ascendancy or dominance. In critical scholarship, hegemonic struggle refers to the struggle over civil society and the state waged by different classes and cultural groups. The most influential theorist of this conception of hegemony was Italian philosopher and social theorist **Antonio Gramsci**.

Gramsci was a Marxist who was imprisoned under Mussolini's Fascist rule in the 1930s. Gramsci broke with other Marxist thinkers of his day who emphasized that the struggle of working-class men and women for a society that represents the interests and views of workers could only be achieved through force or coercion—militant strikes, a violent seizure of state power by a revolutionary party, or economic struggles alone. He also was interested in how the struggle for power was not only about the struggle to control the production of things but also the struggle over ideas, that is, over whose ideas were dominant. Gramsci, too, was committed to revolutionary change in which capitalist exploitation and a class-stratified order could be replaced with a just and democratic political and economic order. However, Gramsci emphasized that while state power is held through force, the holding of state power requires the consent of the governed, which must be won through education. For Gramsci every political relationship was an educational one. To hold power, groups must educate others to its common sense, language, values, and ideology. Struggles for political power for Gramsci centrally involve educating others into one's culture and language and involve winning civil society.

A crucial aspect of Gramsci's thought is the recognition that different classes and groups have their own organic culture and intellectuals. That is, knowledge and ideology are particular to classes despite the fact that the ruling class misframes knowledge as being universal and politically neutral and misframes ideology as being only a distortion of the truth. Gramsci proposed that working-class people needed to develop intellectuals who could articulate social reality through working-class interests and demands. Everyone, for Gramsci, is an intellectual in the sense of being a maker of ideas, but not everyone has the social *role* of an intellectual. He distinguishes between two kinds of intellectuals: **traditional intellectuals** and **organic intellectuals**. Traditional intellectuals produce knowledge and ideology in the service of ruling-class people who need the culture and language to express ways of seeing the world that accord with the maintenance of the existing class order. Traditional intellectuals for Gramsci pose as socially neutral specialized experts, though actually they are not.

Each group (what Gramsci calls "historical bloc," or class-based organization) has its own organic intellectuals: intellectuals who are endemic to its own social position, interests, and values. And in order for a group to gain and hold power, the group needs to develop these organic intellectuals in ways that persuade others to accept that group's ways of seeing the social world. Gramsci writes,

> One of the most important characteristic of any group that is developing towards dominance is its struggle to assimilate and to conquer 'ideologically' the traditional intellectuals, but this assimilation and conquest is made quicker and more efficacious the more the group in question succeeds in simultaneously elaborating its own organic intellectuals. (*Prison Notebooks*, 305)

A leading advocate of critical pedagogy, Henry Giroux, has built on Gramsci's work to suggest that teachers need to understand their roles as intellectuals in the forging of a more democratic society through the inevitable practices that they do as intellectuals in classrooms. In his book *Teachers as Intellectuals*, Giroux distinguishes between traditional intellectuals, **critical intellectuals**, and **transformative intellectuals**. Traditional intellectuals largely serve powerful economic and political elites as makers of culture and knowledge. Critical intellectuals take up knowledge in relation to questions of power and politics but do not link such analyses to action or foster in students forms of agency that would create conditions for critical knowledge to be transformative. Transformative intellectuals both link knowledge to power and politics and foster action and political agency.

The Poverty of "Good" Suburban Schooling

Conservative, liberal, and even progressive education authors put on a pedestal the allegedly good schools of rich communities in the suburbs. Dominant educational policy likewise positions these schools as idealized models for urban and rural schools in poor communities. In this view, the test scores of the rich schools prove their superiority and justify educational reforms in poor schools that would never be implemented in rich schools, such as heavy discipline, rigid approaches to instruction, didactic and anti-dialogical forms of teaching, standardization, and the devaluing of students' identities, cultures, language, and experiences. Gramsci's perspective complicates this picture by suggesting that the knowledge and culture of the schools of the rich should be understood less as representative of universally valuable knowledge and culture and more as the knowledge, culture, and ideology of the ruling group. If this is the case, then the demands for adherence to this falsely universalized knowledge, ideology, and culture would be a political move that not only sets all but the ruling groups up for failure but also imposes the dominant group's common sense upon subordinate groups. At the same time, the dominant group's techniques for imposing their knowledge marginalize pedagogical approaches that would emphasize the political dimensions of knowledge. So the poverty of "good" schools involves the way they deny students in them the tools to ideologically critique the society they inhabit while these intellectually and politically impoverished schools also become the false ideal for other schools and students deemed inferior.

Gramsci's work insists that the work that teachers do matters in how it enacts the future, forms students as particular kinds of people, and sets the conditions for how people will collectively address public problems. Put differently, Gramsci's work recognizes the inevitable formation of different kinds of **agency** that teachers facilitate in students. Do students learn the tools for ongoing self and social interpretation and intervention, or do they learn habits of thought and action that make them complicit in their own oppression and the oppression of others? Gramsci's work disrupts the traditional category of the intellectual as aligned with the false neutrality and universality of the disinterested scholar. It also challenges the anti-intellectualism of much activism, instead insisting that those struggling for emancipatory change need to be able to theorize and historicize situations. For Gramsci, social groups struggle for social ascendancy in part through the wielding of force but also through the winning of consent of other groups. That is, any group that has won social power has managed to educate other groups into particular ways of thinking and acting. Politics is primarily educational.

Why It Matters Now

Gramsci understood the struggle for working men and women to achieve dominance as being primarily one limited to the terrain of the nation-state, and he also saw the political party as being the primary vehicle for this struggle. While Gramsci's insights are crucial to understanding hegemonic struggles, his nationally bounded and political party–based conception of political change needs to be expanded as these struggles become increasingly global. Of particular importance is the ongoing role of teachers as necessarily makers of knowledge and culture and their necessarily political role as organic intellectuals and permanent persuaders. As well, schools are no longer the primary pedagogical force in society, having been surpassed by the pedagogical power of mass media, which is also global in its reach. Gramsci differed from other Marxists of his day who saw culture and civil society as being secondary to the economy. Gramsci understood that culture and civil society are not only crucial terrains of struggle for competing social groups but also that material struggles only make sense within cultures. Gramsci recognized that power is wielded not only through coercion (such as through the use of weapons and the power to strike and shut down production). Power is wielded through the making of ideas and meanings, through educating people to consent to particular ways of seeing.

There are enormous implications for educators of understanding the theory of hegemony and Gramsci's conception of the role of intellectuals. First, he conceived of education as inherently political. Today's public problems include environmental destruction so severe that scientists now question the possibility of the survival of the human species, not to mention most others. The environmental crisis is not primarily a technical problem to be solved but rather a matter of social values, vision for the future, and political will. In order to address this public problem, citizens need to be educated to understand that capitalism and its imperative for unchecked pursuit of profit results in the pillage of nature. Profit cannot be relied upon to solve the problems that profiteering has created. To create the widespread understanding and political will to tackle this crucial problem requires educational projects. Forms of education that delink learning from problems in the world are nonetheless political by affirming existing realities and structures of power. Instead, public problems demand forms of learning that help students comprehend how they are oppressed by broader forces and institutions and how such understanding can form the basis for changing these forces and institutions in emancipatory ways.

Public problems today include the roll back of the gains of the civil rights movement of the 1950s, 1960s, and 1970s with efforts for racial and ethnic equality, problems ranging from the resegregation of schools to voter suppression. The de facto system of racial segregation structuring schools, real estate, and work institutions can only remain in place as people are continually educated to accept such arrangements. Gramsci's emphasis on struggles over culture and civil society and his refusal of economism mean that he makes it necessary to comprehend how power blocs cannot be comprehended singularly through only questions of racial identity or ethnic identity or only through questions of class; instead, groups struggling for social ascendancy are forged through multiple sutured-together positions—class, race, ethnicity, sexuality, and so on. The realities of these identity positions is made meaningful in part through the others and also by being defined against the identity positions that are excluded from the group. For example, a normative politics of emancipation must be defined against identities defined through hierarchical social organization or authoritarianism or anti-democratic politics. If, as Gramsci reminds us, we are all involved in doing intellectual work, then the question is: what kinds of intellectual work do teachers and administrators do toward making a new kind of common sense oriented around freedom and equality? Any effort at an emancipatory politics by transformative intellectuals requires linking multiple struggles against oppression and for common benefit.

Public problems also include the political authoritarianism that has been rapidly expanding in the United States and around the world. A commitment to equality and democracy must be taught and learned. Radically worsened inequalities in wealth and income have been accompanied by the drastic erosion of civil liberties, the overtaking of the representative electoral system by moneyed elites, and a crisis of journalism, news, and information caused by extreme corporate consolidation of ownership over mass media. At the same time educational reform has been radically subject to the forces of privatization as public schooling has been seen as one of the last enormous public sectors that the private sector can pillage for profit. Students are being seen by investors as lucrative commodities for companies managing schools for profit and for test publishing companies. These public problems require public responses from an educated citizenry capable of interpretation and social intervention.

The new educational reforms grounded in market metaphors and corporate culture—such as the heavy emphasis on standardized testing and standardization of curriculum, scripted lessons, and direct instruction—undermine pedagogical approaches that link knowledge to power, politics, and ethics. That is, the intellectual tools that students need to interpret and contextualize claims to truth are undermined by the current reforms that treat knowledge as a consumable commodity and that reduce questions of understanding to only that which is measurable and quantifiable. If teachers and students are to struggle collectively for greater justice, more egalitarian social relationships, and to address the most crucial public problems such as authoritarianism, ecological crisis, and consumerism, then they need to not only learn to model democracy in schools and classrooms but also to link what goes on in schools to what goes on in the world.

Suggested Further Reading

Antonio Gramsci. *Selections from the Prison Notebooks.* New York: International Publishers, 1971.

Gramsci asserted that the struggle for power was not only about the struggle to control the production of things but also the struggle over ideas. He was committed to revolutionary change in which capitalist exploitation and a class-stratified order could be replaced with a just and democratic political and economic order. However, Gramsci emphasized that while state power is held through force, the holding of state power requires the consent of the governed, which must be won through education.

Henry Giroux. *Teachers as Intellectuals: Towards a Critical Pedagogy of Learning.* Westport, CT: Bergin & Garvey, 1988.

Giroux expands Gramsci's distinction between different kinds of intellectuals distinguishing traditional from critical from transformative intellectuals. The crucial difference between critical and transformative intellectuals is that the former explicate on politics and power while the latter link their analyses to efforts for social change. In the U.S. context of treating teachers as practitioners, and a longer history of anti-intellectualism, Giroux's project of treating teachers as socially engaged intellectuals could not be more important.

Michael Apple. *Ideology and Curriculum.* New York: Routledge, 1977.

Apple explains Gramsci's concept of hegemony and situates it in terms of U.S. schooling and the critical sociology of knowledge.

Questions for Discussion

1. What are the two senses of hegemony laid out here?
2. What is the difference between traditional intellectuals and organic intellectuals?
3. What does Giroux's distinction between traditional, critical, and transformative intellectuals add to Gramsci?
4. What is at stake in distinguishing the kinds of intellectuals as opposed to accepting the dominant explanation of one kind of intellectual?
5. How is politics always educational according to the theory of hegemony?
6. How is education always political according to the theory of hegemony?

Chapter Five
Disciplinary Power, Race, and Examinations

This chapter explains Foucault's concepts of disciplinary power, normalization, and the examination, analyzing them in relation to contemporary trends in standardized testing, the making of students into cases, and the differential making of racialized subjects through school discipline: the idea of the "achievement gap" and racially segregated corporate school reform.

Disciplinary Power

French social philosopher **Michel Foucault** reconceptualized power, emphasizing the extent to which knowledge-making is always interwoven with power relations. Foucault believed that most social philosophies, including those developed through Marx, imagined power as top-down, that is, as always operating onto subjects that already existed before powers operations and outside of them. Power worked through constraining those under its jurisdiction. Foucault instead believed that these social philosophies were starting from the wrong premises and that power actually brought subjects into existence and that, through bringing subjects into existence, power constituted itself. Subjects got their life, he believed, when institutions called them into being or made a place for them. Foucault's conception of power emphasizes that power works predominately not through *restriction* but rather through *producing* knowledge and **subject positions**.

Power, for Foucault, should be thought of as originating at the local level and generated by practices and rituals in institutions. Foucault's histories of various institutions such as the prison, the mental asylum, and the hospital show how what he calls "modern power" differs from the wielding of power in the "classical age." In the classical age, Foucault explains, power was wielded in specific places where examples were made—spectacles of punishment on the body like public executions. In the modern age, power is everywhere, seamless, networked, and involves everyone, operating through surveillance and connected to life instead of death. In his book *Discipline and Punish*, for example, Foucault paints a vivid picture of the difference between state punishment in the classical age of monarchy and pre-capitalist economic formations as opposed to the modern form of punishment found after the advent of capitalism and parliamentary democracy.

Foucault recounts the classical age drawing and quartering of "Damien the Regicide" by the sovereign. The prisoner is put on display for the commoners to watch the fate of those who would dare to challenge the power of the king. Foucault contrasts this gory picture with the prison of the nineteenth century, which was characterized by intense control over time and space. Prisoners in this system followed a strict schedule and were under surveillance by the guards. Early prisons follow a design of the **panopticon** that puts cells around a central tower, allowing guards to potentially watch the prisoners at any moment. Prisoners quickly learn that because they may be watched at any time, they must watch themselves, leading to a kind of learned self-regulation. Power in the modern age for Foucault involves reversed relations of looking. Everyone increasingly becomes subject to a new kind of insidious power of being under surveillance and being put in positions to have supervision over others who are in subordinate positions. This logic of surveillance can be found in numerous modern institutions, for Foucault, ranging from the prison to the military, the asylum, the hospital, and the school.

Foucault's account of modern disciplinary power emphasizes how particular social relations are produced through the micropractices and micropolitics of everyday life. Power originates in the rituals and practices that people do in institutions. Foucault's picture of power displaces a traditional picture of power as top-down, hierarchical, and always looming outside. For example, the Marxian tradition sees the power of economic oppression as a large structural determining force. Within the Marxian tradition knowledge is an effect of the social force that really matters: the material relations of production, that is, the economy. Knowledge in the Marxian view is either a correct reflection of that reality or a distortion coming under the same ideology. For Foucault, knowledge is always a form of power, and power is "implicated in the questions of whether and in what circumstances knowledge is to be applied or not."[1] The liberal philosophical tradition posits the power of great men and ideas and the force of the state as the large external origins of the power that matters. Foucault does not deny these sources of power, but he emphasizes how in the modern age with the decline of aristocracy and serfdom power retrenches and is wielded in subtler ways. Disciplinary power is composed of normalizing judgment and hierarchical surveillance.

Normalizing judgment involves comparing, differentiating, ranking, measuring against a norm, homogenizing, and standardizing. Hierarchical surveillance involves the watching of individuals to judge them in terms of these various norms. Take, for example, the normalizing judgment that is applied to soldiers in the modern military. Soldiers are paraded on an exercise field and subject to examination by an officer who stands above them. The soldiers are examined for how well they have dressed themselves and how well they move their bodies in prescribed fashion. The soldiers are compared with each other; they are differentiated by their conformity to the norms of military ritual and through comparison to each other and an ideal. Foucault emphasizes that the importance of disciplinary power is that it induces people through rituals and practices to make themselves into particular kinds of subjects through the inwardly turned gaze. People learn to regulate themselves and their conduct.

Likewise, in the modern school the student is also subject to the hierarchical surveillance of the teacher and the teacher subject to the hierarchical surveillance of the administration. The student is subject to examination (sometimes visual inspection, sometimes tests) that again compares, differentiates, ranks, measures against a norm, and homogenizes and standardizes. Again, for Foucault, the crucial aspect of this form of power is the way that individuals, by participating in the rituals of the institution, make themselves into particular kinds of self-regulating persons or subjects. The physical arrangement of the classroom participates in hierarchical surveillance. The teacher sits facing students while the students all face the teacher to be watched. The standardized examination is applied to students while the person or people who made the test are absent from the classroom; modern power is invisible. Students are subject to being measured against the norm produced by comparison with other students.

With the expansion of teacher pay for performance and so-called value-added assessment in which teacher quality is made a function of student test scores, teachers are subject to greater and greater disciplinary power as well. Foucault insists that disciplinary power works like a web. Individuals are subject to hierarchical surveillance and also made agents of hierarchical surveillance on those below in the institution. In working-class and poor schools, students are subject to the forms of disciplinary surveillance more typically associated with the prison. Closed-circuit television, body-scanning devices, and police presence are common in these schools. Foucault helps us understand that these mechanisms do not simply react to people who are already formed as people. Instead, these disciplinary surveillance devices actively produce individuals in particular ways. Working-class and poor students are being educated through these techniques to think of themselves through the lens and assumptions of criminality and exclusion from the dominant institutions of the society.

Disciplining the Black Student Body

In her book *Bad Boys*, Ann Arnette Ferguson draws on both critical pedagogy and Foucault's thought to illustrate how in urban schools populated by working-class and poor African American students, discipline is not simply applied in reaction to the behaviors of students. As Ferguson explains, students are produced as particular kinds of racialized and disciplined subjects by how they are subject to being watched, spoken to, and positioned in the institution of the school and how they are positioned by reference to implicit norms including norms of whiteness. Such norms of whiteness link racialized signs such as skin color to behavioral practices.

> A defiant, challenging, oppositional body; dramatic, emotional expressions; a rich, complex nonstandard vocabulary establish the "outer limits" in a field of comparison in which the desired norm is a docile bodily presence and the intonation and homogeneous syntax of Standard English. This outer limit is exemplified by the black child: the closer to whiteness, to the norm of bodies, language, emotion, the more these children *are* self-disciplined and acceptable members of the institution. (Ferguson, 72)

The African American children that Ferguson observes in her field study of a school are not merely presumed to be "bad" by the adult disciplinarians.

In other words, being made into bad boys and bad girls is not only a matter of a self-fulfilling prophecy. It is also a matter of how particular physical traits are symbolically aligned with social meanings such as the black male body and fear.

Foucault's and Ferguson's analyses of how power works through discipline complicate the meaning-making practices of teachers. Such meaning-making practices must here be understood as always implicated in affirming or challenging existing relations of power and sets of meanings. Moreover, their discussions ask us to revise our understanding of what goes on in schools as a response to pre-existing authentic student and teacher identities. Rather, they suggest that schools are not simply places where knowledge is transferred but rather that schools are places where student identities are made, often in unequal and oppressive fashion.

The Possibilities of Resistance

Foucault's perspective offered a new and also problematic conception of student resistance. Educational sociologists in the 1970s and 1980s in the United States and United Kingdom such as Paul Willis, Angela McRobbie, Henry Giroux, and others sought to understand how students' creative resistance to oppressive institutions such as schools both subverted those students' own life chances and yet might also hold the means for oppositional social movements to be developed. Critical educational scholars imagined the possibility for student resistance against oppressive forces assuming the possibility for autonomous student agency and the possibility for the development of critical forms of consciousness. Foucault's conception of resistance introduces the problem that since power constitutes us, every time we speak or act, we are in a sense reconfirming power. There is no separation between subjects who are constituted by power and the apparatus of power itself—no possibility of a distance from or an outside to power. So a resistant act is both a reconfirmation of the apparatus of power that constitutes us as much as an opposition. Foucault's example of the homosexual is a good one: in the nineteenth century, the Victorian repression of sexuality through the institutions of the church, the school, and the medical clinic produced the identity of the homosexual as an identity constituted through its repression. In the 1960s, this repressed identity became a source of power and opposition; as it was constituted through power, it exploded on the political scene as an expression of power as the gay and lesbian movement was born. Foucault's conceptualization of resistance raises this question: To what extent are other types of identities able to assume power through constraint? Does this example translate more generally?

Theoretical Problems with Foucauldian Power

Foucault's way of conceptualizing power, while valuable, has serious limitations. As **Nancy Fraser** has argued, for example, he refused to put forward ethical and political norms from which to justify his own criticisms of oppressive power and from which to ground normative social values. Such norms might have included equality and human rights. Foucault's refusal to do so was based in his contention that particular values are historically constituted and made intelligible through power. Norms cannot be seen as universal or outside of the forces of power through which they are brought to life. (For those interested in this question, see Jürgen Habermas's discussion of Foucault in *The Philosophical Discourse of Modernity* or the *Chomsky Foucault Debate.*) What we can draw from Fraser's insistence on the inevitability of norms is that if teachers are going to engage in critical practices in schools they need to be cognizant of the values and ideologies that they accept and champion through their daily practices. Moreover, if schools are places that produce subject positions from which students become individuals, then teachers have a large role and a great responsibility for reflecting upon what kinds of subject positions they are implicated in producing for youth.

Fraser offers an additional more recent criticism of Foucault. Foucault's theory of disciplinary power, which focused on learned self-regulation, became popular in U.S. universities at an economic and social moment of tremendous change. Economically the United States was shifting from a **Fordist** industrial production economy to a **post-Fordist** post-industrial service economy. As Fraser explains, the regulation of the self and the society shifted with the change in the economy. While learned self-regulation was an apt mode of social control for industry and industry's compact with a **welfare state** form of government, the new economy of **neoliberalism** since the 1970s increasingly shifted the onus of economic responsibility to individuals while governments systematically scaled back social spending on the safety net. Consequently, as Fraser argues, the regulation of individuals has taken an increasingly individualized form that accords with selves as primarily economic actors: individuals are expected to be adroit consumers and entrepreneurial subjects.

As Fraser explains, social regulation in a post-Fordist economy depends less and less on time- and labor-intensive strategies of learned self-regulation described by Foucault's theory of disciplinary power. Instead, social regulation depends on an increasingly dual society in which the shrinking professional class learns to compete in a precarious economy and the rest of the society is subject to greater and greater forms of repression and direct bodily control. Mental illness is less and less treated through the time- and labor-intensive talk therapy of psychoanalysis and increasingly through bodily control with pharmacology. Increasingly privatized prisons are less about rehabilitation through learned self-regulation and more about control of bodies. As **Zygmunt Bauman** describes, in California's Pelican Bay Prison Foucault's panopticon has given way to the synopticon in which nobody cares what the prisoner does—what matters is the locking away of the prisoners' body. The same could be said of the prisoners at Guantanamo, whose prisoners are afforded no legal process, much less any attempts at rehabilitation.

This shift in contemporary forms of control pertains to the direction that school reform has taken in the past decade. Schools of the working class and poor have become increasingly repressive, being modeled on prisons or the military. The new corporate school reforms and their most popular pedagogical approaches favor rigid, directive, scripted lessons and standardization of time and space. Corporate nonprofit KIPP and the for-profit management company Edison Learning, both among the largest private managers of schools, typify these repressive approaches to teaching and learning with a heavy emphasis on bodily control, eyes on the teacher, feet flat on the floor, and punishments for deviation from the norm. This bodily and pedagogical repression targets disproportionately black and brown poor students in urban areas. These schools presume that students are to be subject to heavy discipline, and this discipline is framed as being in the students' best interests for economic competition. Increasingly, these schools are privatized, turning poor students of color into investment opportunities for a small number of predominantly white rich people.

Meanwhile, schools of the professional class remain largely public and treat predominantly white students very differently despite the same rhetoric about economic competition. These students are expected to take the managerial leadership role in the economy and accordingly are engaged more in dialogue and less subject to scripted monologue. They are given greater latitude for movement and speaking up and participating, needing to learn "entrepreneurial" forms of self-regulation. Yet, in accord with Fraser's and Bauman's insights, learned self-regulation is joined by direct bodily control as in the heavy use of pharmaceuticals to medicate students into attention for education competition on tests. We are witnessing the expansion of what French philosopher Gilles Deleuze termed "societies of control" in which the direct control of bodies and populations becomes paramount. Yet, in contemporary neoliberal education reform such direct coercion intersects with Foucault's disciplinary power of learned self-regulation typified by testing, surveillance, and so on.

Corporate school reforms such as chartering, privatization, vouchers, and high-stakes standardized testing assume that so-called market discipline ought to be merged with bodily and behavioral discipline. This assumption is highly racialized and racist for several reasons. First, these policies and practices fail to challenge the legacy of racial segregation in traditional public schooling and, in fact, they exacerbate racial segregation. It is not only through segregation that corporate school reforms promote a racist form of discipline. This is also done discursively by misframing educational problems. Standardized testing and standardization of curriculum allege neutrality with regard to culture, race, ethnicity, and language. In this view, cultural difference is positioned as a problem only to be overcome. For example, the so-called problem of an **achievement gap** that is attributed to blacks and latinos as a deficit denies cultural difference in terms of curriculum, pedagogy, and cultural politics of knowledge. Difference is to be registered only as a cause of failure to reach the quantifiable norm. At the same time, the norm is denied as being particular to any cultural group or class.

Conclusion

Foucault's work, as well as Ferguson's, Fraser's, and Bauman's, offers teachers and others theoretical tools, language, and concepts that can be selectively appropriated to interpret school situations, policies, and practices. Corporate school reforms worsen the historical racial and ethnic segregation of the public system, they worsen the radical funding inequalities of the public school system, and they worsen some of the anti-intellectual and anti-critical tendencies of the public school system. Teachers and administrators can draw on these and other theories in efforts to imagine and create a new, better public school system that is integrated, fairly financed, and critically intellectual in its pedagogy and curriculum. Such efforts for remaking of schools can be seen as part of a broader collective effort for the making of a thoughtful and compassionate society. If, as Fraser suggests, our practices always aspire toward particular normative political and ethical values, then it is incumbent upon teachers to reflect upon the broader values animating their pedagogical practices and the ways that practices enact a vision for the future.

Suggested Further Reading

Michel Foucault. *Discipline and Punish: The Birth of the Prison*. New York: Vintage, 1977.

Foucault's book explains how the practice of an institution becomes self-regulating.

Ann Arnett Ferguson. *Bad Boys: Public Schools in the Making of Black Masculinity*. Ann Arbor: University of Michigan Press, 2001.

An application of Foucault's prison theory to education that shows how repressive school practices contribute to the creation of black male identity.

Nancy Fraser. *Unruly Practices*. Minneapolis: University of Minnesota Press, 1989.

Fraser's volume includes a critique of Foucault's theory of power, especially Foucault's refusal to base his theory in a principle like human rights.

Nancy Fraser. "From Discipline to Flexibilization: Rereading Foucault in the Shadow of Globalization." *Constellations* 2002.

Fraser continues her critique of Foucault's theory of power.

Zygmunt Bauman. *Globalization: The Human Consequences*. New York: Polity, 1998.

Bauman's book includes an update on prison methods.

Henry Giroux. *Theory and Resistance in Education*. Westport, CT: Bergin & Garvey, 1983.

Giroux's classic work contains an early criticism of Foucault's conception of power.

Paul Willis. *Learning to Labor*. New York: Routledge, 1977.

Willis's ethnographic study of British youth was influential on theories of student opposition and resistance. It argued that domination is never total and that students mediate and live out class in contradictory ways. It also made the case that much student opposition becomes the basis for the class oppression and subjugation of these youth throughout life.

Gloria Ladson-Billings. "Pushing Past the Achievement Gap: An Essay on the Language of Deficit." *The Journal of Negro Education* 76, no. 3 (2007): 316–323.

This article investigates the ways that the creation of invisible norms are universalized and used to pathologize minority youth.

Questions for Discussion

1. How does Foucault's conception of power differ from that of the Marxian tradition?
2. What is normalizing judgment, and how is it deployed in schools?
3. What is hierarchical surveillance, and how is it deployed in schools?
4. How do Foucault's concepts help to understand the racism that structures public schooling and potentially contribute to anti-racist pedagogies?
5. How can teachers and administrators contribute to the making of "bad boys" rather than simply responding to them?
6. What are Fraser's two criticisms of Foucault's reconceptualization of power?
7. Why is the idea of an achievement gap problematic, and how is it political?

Note

1. Stuart Hall, *Representation: Cultural Representations and Signifying Practices* (Thousand Oaks, CA: Sage, 1997), 48.

Chapter Six
Biopolitics and Education

This chapter discusses the different versions of biopolitics (or regulatory power) as the production and management of populations and the management of life and death. It looks at recent uses in education to understand the making of disposable populations, the culture of control throughout education, "lifelong learning," and the ways that the increasing corporate control over education invades the body and the body politic.

What Is Biopolitics?

Biopolitics refers to a form of politics in which the production and management of life dominates. We live at a time in which not just nature but life itself can be made and manipulated like information, patented, and owned. Genetics allows scientists to merge species, while the biological integration of animals, humans, and machines has become increasingly possible. The Enlightenment dream of the mastery of nature through the use of science and technology has been integral to capitalist accumulation, and together these projects, unrivaled in history, have made possible comforts, luxuries, and security for vast numbers of people. Yet the technical domination of nature and profit-seeking also produce ecological devastation, poverty, desperation, and dire human insecurity for half of the planet's population and the possibility of global nuclear annihilation under nuclear fallout.

Human-caused global warming and the forced migrations it will produce, the drastic transformations to nature through industrial means, and the vast impact of growing populations on eco-stability mean that nature can no longer be understood as truly separate from humanity. The planet is being managed by, impacted by, and destroyed by human beings with the introduction of vast chemicals, species extinctions, and pollution. In fact, human beings have for more than half a century held the capacity for near total destruction of living species through global nuclear Armageddon and global climate change.

Schools are a place where future citizens can learn to better manage and steward a nature that is becoming more closely integrated with the human. Yet, in current trends to vocationalize schooling through so-called STEM subjects (science, technology, engineering, and mathematics), learning is being delinked from the social implications of these technical subjects. By falsely positioning the sciences as neutral, apolitical, and merely technical, these subjects are presumed to be valuable for their market applications. Yet the promises of wealth and productivity gains are often unfulfilled, and the unfettered use of technology continues to degrade the environment while sacrificing true scientific knowledge and the public interest.

In recent years, the environmental movement has focused on individual choices like turning off lightbulbs, conserving energy in the home, and limiting excessive consumption and waste. But the true driving force of environmental destruction has been the profit-seeking activities of large corporations and the power-seeking behavior of governments acting in large part on behalf of monied interests. The new field of biopolitics recognizes that politics has great impact on populations and even the production of new forms of living. Theories of biopolitics offer a lens on politics that rejects individualistic approaches to ecology and life science yet it goes beyond explaining the actions of the powerful to control the rest of the population.

A Shift in Sovereignty

Michel Foucault explains biopolitics in part through a historical shift in **sovereignty** in which the historical right over life and death as the dominant wielding of power cedes to more contemporary forms of power "that seeks to administer, secure, develop, and foster life" (Lemke, 2011). Formal schooling, for example, plays a central role in the active production of particular kinds of subjects (selves) that accord with the interests of states and industry. The state seeks to produce subjects who will submit to a civil rule, while industry seeks to produce docile and compliant workers for low-pay, low-skill jobs. Of course, governments and businesses also require leaders and need to produce creative problem solvers for the leadership roles in the economy and in the government.

The role of schools in producing the various types of workers is crucial to the sorting and sifting of populations. For example, the allegedly neutral standardized testing process subjects each student to hierarchical observation by an unseen examiner (the ones who made the tests). Each student must perform the truth about him or herself by doing the test and displaying progress toward a standardized norm of "performance."

Producing Knowledge of Life

Thomas Lemke in his book *Biopolitics: An Advanced Introduction* suggests three important dimensions of biopolitics that I want to expand upon with regard to the contemporary politics of education. First, biopolitics involves the making of a knowledge of life. Lemke writes,

> One must ask what knowledge of the body and life processes is assumed to be socially relevant and, by contrast, what alternative interpretations are devalued or marginalized. What scientific experts and disciplines have legitimate authority to tell the truth about life, health, or a given population? In what vocabulary are processes of life described, measured, evaluated, and criticized? What cognitive and intellectual instruments and technological procedures stand ready to produce truth? What proposals and definitions of problems and objectives regarding processes of life are given social recognition? (119)

The current craze for standardized testing and standardization of curriculum obviously participates in devaluing unique aspects of an individual child. Such tests work by putting a focus on those aspects of experience that can be empirically measured and numerically quantified, that is, on that which can be controlled.

Which scientific authorities have increasing legitimacy to "tell the truth" about the lives of students and teachers? Economists, business people without educational expertise, test makers, and publishers increasingly have become authorized to educate the broader public about educational values, largely through the lens of profit-seeking. As making students foremost into workers and consumers has become a hegemonic value, experts in these domains have become authorized to speak the truth about youth and educational reform, while the vocabulary of business has become increasingly the vocabulary of educational improvement. What makes someone a good teacher? Inspiring curiosity and creative thought in students? No, raising numerical test scores. What makes somebody a good student? A disposition for reasoned judgment and dialogue, for relating claims to truth to historical power struggles and social and ethical matters? No, scoring high numerical test scores. The very idea of what it means to live a good life (to compete against others to sell one's labor power to someone who can buy it in order to buy luxury goods) gets defined through the assumptions of these specialists and "regimes of truth."

There are countless other ways that the making of the "truth" of groups of people has vast political and ethical implications. For example, adolescents are described and subjected to school policy based on nineteenth-century ideas about the "storm and stress" and "raging hormones" of the adolescent body (see, for example, Brown and Saltman's *Critical Middle School Reader* in the suggested reading list). More recently, educational competition structured by the assumptions of economic competition legitimizes the use of pharmaceutical drugs for educational competition on standardized tests. Here, the naturalized "truth" of that knowledge deemed important on standardized tests joins with the naturalized "truth" of a social world defined by **social Darwinian** competition in the economy and the "truth" of the necessity for managed self-regulation of the body for this competition with the help of amphetamines like Adderall.

Lemke emphasizes that because "the problem of the regime of truth cannot be separated from that of power, the question arises of how strategies of power mobilize knowledge of life and how processes of power generate and disseminate forms of knowledge" (119). The "truth" of different groups is continually produced through institutionalized practices, and these knowledges have real material effects to determine life chances, standards of living, and opportunity. For example, standardized tests, which are alleged to be neutral and of universal value, are used to hierarchically position different populations such as different racial, ethnic, linguistic groups, and genders and set them up for different incomes and standards of living. The "truth" produced about working-class and poor people and nonwhite people through crime entertainment and news programs in the institutions of mass media has material effects in disparate treatment in the criminal justice systems.

Making Subjects

Lemke emphasizes a third dimension of biopolitics having to do with identity formation:

> An analytics of biopolitics must also take into account forms of subjectivation, that is, the manner in which subjects are brought to work on themselves, guided by scientific, medical, moral, religious, and other authorities and on the basis of socially accepted arrangements of bodies and sexes. . . . How are people called on, in the name of (individual and collective) life and health (one's own health and that of the family, nation, "race," and so forth), in view of defined goals (health improvement, life extension, higher quality of life, amelioration of the gene pool, population increase, and so forth) to act in a certain way (in extreme cases even to die for such goals)? How are they brought to experience their life as "worthy" or "not worthy" of being lived? How are they **interpellated** as members of a "higher" or "inferior" race, a "strong" or a "weak" sex, a "rising" or a "degenerate" people? (120)

Lemke's questions point to some obvious ways that students are made in very different particular ways in schools—ways that can result in some students living and other students dying.

For example, it is not a coincidence that while working-class and poor students and students of color are shunted toward war fighting in overseas escapades, professional-class white students are shunted toward university and the safety and security of professional work. Students are not mobilized in these very different directions through coercion. Rather, students learn that their lives are supposed to take particular directions and that the good or bad fortune that they have has to do with their own alleged natural abilities rather than a social structure and sociological patterns that privilege certain groups over others. In other words, a crucial yet largely false lesson that all students learn in school is that their place in the social order has to do with their own capacities as individuals rather than with the sorting and sifting mechanisms in place to unequally distribute life chances.

Much of how this is accomplished is through the sometimes overt and sometimes subtle lessons that students learn about their own language, culture, and group, and how these pieces of their identity relate to the rest of those in society. Professional-class and working-class students are now subjected to the ideology of corporate culture that demands that individuals learn to be successful entrepreneurial subjects. This means learning to compete educationally in order to later compete economically in the labor market. For professional-class students the power and profits of the medical industries is profoundly involved in medicating students into sustained attention on the consumption of meaningless and decontextualized knowledge toward the end of educational competition on tests. Increasingly working-class and poor students find that they are made into criminalized subjects by the ways that the prison institutions and industries participate in schooling from security apparatus to the structuring of teacher attitudes in schools. As the economy renders more and more youth economically redundant for the future, these youth enter the school-to-prison pipeline and on the way become the means for corporate profits in the school management industries. We see in these examples the convergence of the making of particular truths about youth, the convergence of these regimes of truth with power and institutions, and the formation of subjectivities. But individuals are hardly a mere effect of dominant biopower.

An Egalitarian and Emancipatory Biopolitics?

Henry Giroux's recent work on biopolitics highlights the theoretical limitations of various theories of biopolitics in terms of the current social realities of neoliberalism and the making of disposable populations—that is, the cruel social abandonment of economically redundant populations accompanying the neoliberal gutting of the caregiving roles of the state. He argues in *Youth in a Suspect Society* that theories of biopolitics must eschew **fatalistic** and **deterministic** tendencies and instead be linked to the ongoing and inevitable educational work that people do inside and outside of formal schooling as well as the inevitable making of particular kinds of agency. Giroux's work demonstrates that there are far more egalitarian and emancipatory truths that can be told about youth and society than those in the examples above. He concludes his chapter "In the Shadow of the Gilded Age: Biopolitics in the Age of Disposability" by stating,

> Any politics that takes seriously a society's ethical and political obligations to the young demands more than the production of critical knowledge and a commitment to social justice. It also suggests an ongoing struggle to create the pedagogical conditions and political sites/public spheres in which alliances can be built and global movements initiated as part of a broader effort to create new **modes of identification, political subjectivities, social relations of resistance**, and sources of mobilization dedicated to making the world a more humane and

> just space for all children. Biopolitics in the interest of a global democracy is a struggle over those modes of state and corporate sovereignty that control the means of life and death. (Giroux, 2010, 187–188)

Through their daily practices teachers are involved in producing truths about youth, informing the formation of youth subjectivities, and affirming or contesting the alignment of institutional power with these regimes of truth. Consequently teachers ought to reflect upon what values and principles guide these choices and actions and link their reflective practices to a vision of justice for the future.

Suggested Further Reading

Henry Giroux. *Youth in a Suspect Society: Democracy or Disposability?* New York: Palgrave, 2010.

An important addition to the literature of biopolitics that emphasizes our ability to be actors within the dehumanizing biopolitical system.

Kenneth J. Saltman. *Capitalizing on Disaster: Taking and Breaking Public Schools.* Boulder, CO: Paradigm, 2007.

This book examines how natural and human disasters have been used to privatize and corporatize public schooling internationally. It examines how populations have been dispossessed of homes and schools explaining the discursive uses of business language to accomplish this.

Clayton Pierce. *Education in the Age of Biocapitalism.* New York: Palgrave Macmillan, 2013.

Pierce discusses how the science industries are involved in producing knowledge and subjectivities of youth.

Thomas Lemke. *Biopolitics: An Advanced Introduction.* New York: NYU Press, 2011.

Lemke's volume is one of the key texts of biopolitical studies.

Michel Foucault. *Security, Territory, Population: Lectures at the College de France 1977–1978.* New York: Palgrave Macmillan, 2009.

These lectures by Foucault comprise much of the foundation for the contemporary theory on biopolitics.

Michel Foucault. *The Birth of Biopolitics: Lectures at the College de France 1978–1979.* New York: Palgrave Macmillan, 2010.

These lectures by Foucault also comprise much of the foundation for the contemporary theory on biopolitics.

Michel Foucault. *History of Sexuality, Vol. I.* New York: Vintage, 1980.

This volume offers one of the earliest elaborations on biopolitics.

Gilles Deleuze. "Postscript on Societies of Control." In *Cultural Theory,* eds. Imre Szeman and Timothy Kaposy. New York: Wiley, 2010.

This short essay by Deleuze takes up biopolitics in relation to the corporatization of education. While it is valuable, it does not make distinctions between the varieties of control: economic, political, and cultural. Consequently it tends to position power as total while effacing the disjunctures where resistance is possible.

Enora Brown and Kenneth Saltman. *The Critical Middle School Reader.* New York: Routledge, 2005.

This volume includes an elaboration of the politics and social construction of the truth of adolescence.

Henry A. Giroux. *Youth in a Suspect Society: Democracy or Disposability?* New York: Palgrave Macmillan, 2010.

Questions for Discussion

1. Why does the politics of education need to be concerned with the management and making of life?
2. What experts, language, and technologies produce the truth about youth?
3. How are youth made into particular kinds of subjects or selves through regimes of truth?
4. What are some of the struggles that are being waged over the meanings about youth and teachers?

CHAPTER SEVEN
NEOLIBERALISM AND CORPORATE SCHOOL REFORM

This chapter explains how neoliberalism as ideology and economic doctrine is a form of class warfare. It shows how market sovereignty has been restructuring educational policy and practice for thirty years. It then details how neoliberalism is a radical politics that has rapidly undermined liberal and cultural conservative perspectives on schooling while threatening the possibility for the formation of critical forms of education.

What Is Neoliberalism?

Neoliberalism is both an economic doctrine and a cultural ideology. As an economic doctrine, neoliberalism calls for the **privatization** of public goods and services, including education, and deregulation of government controls over markets and labor. Neoliberalism also promotes **trade liberalization**, the opening of national economies to **foreign direct investment** in ways that benefit rich nations and exploit the poor. It favors fiscal policies in rich nations designed to shift economic activity away from production and toward **financialization** and **monetarist policy** that aims for low inflation and economic growth before full employment and higher wages, to benefit investors.

Neoliberalism represents a break with the Keynesian orthodoxy that reigned until the 1970s in which government spending on public sector goods and services and government stimulation of the consumer base were assumed to be necessary to counter the vicissitudes of capitalist markets. Neoliberalism in theory has been very different from neoliberalism in practice. For example, despite the neoliberal rhetoric about the need to shrink big government, right-wing proponents of neoliberal ideology such as Ronald Reagan and George W. Bush presided over radical expansions of federal spending. The crucial shift, however, came in the vast expansion of spending on military and policing and corporate subsidies and the reduction in spending on social services.

Neoliberalism has invested in and fostered the repressive role of the state while whittling away the caregiving role of the state. Neoliberal ideology is dominant in both U.S. mainstream political parties. It was under Democrat Bill Clinton that the dismantling of welfare was accomplished as well as fast-track trade agreements that undermined labor unions. In education, the originally Republican embrace of neoliberal privatization of public schools and the charter school logic of deregulation have been aggressively embraced by many in the Democratic party. Despite the financial crisis and resulting recession brought on by neoliberal deregulation in 2008 and despite the series of economic disasters and radical production of inequality produced through neoliberal restructuring around the world including in Argentina, Thailand, and Chile, the neoliberal dogma has been particularly resilient, especially in education.

In addition to being an economic doctrine, neoliberalism is a cultural ideology. It imagines society as a collection of private individuals who are foremost self-reliant economic agents—that is, workers and consumers. A central aspect of neoliberal ideology has been to encourage individuals to think of themselves in individual and private ways rather than in social and public ways.

Neoliberal Educational Restructuring

Education in the United States has been radically transformed by both the economic doctrine and ideology of neoliberalism. Education has been transformed more through privatization than any other aspect of neoliberal economic doctrine. From the early 1990s, various forms of educational privatization have accelerated, including **school vouchers** (including for parochial and other types of religious schools), **charter schooling**, and **scholarship tax credits**. Vouchers provide individual students with public tax money to pay for private schooling. Vouchers have a troubling history of creating a race to the bottom in which public schools lose their public tax money and decline in quality as a result. The private schools receiving voucher money have a troubling history as well, as private operators of for-profit schools skim money out of operations and the educational process to maximize the difference between the public tax money and the expenditures on educational services. Lastly, vouchers have a troubling history of using public money in a secular government to fund private religious schooling, thereby eroding the separation of church and state in the U.S. Constitution.

Charter schooling uses public tax money to fund schools that remain publicly funded but are privately managed and are less subject to regulations and oversight than district schools. They are justified on the basis of allowing improvements by giving principals greater autonomy to implement experimental changes and on the basis of allowing innovative and experimental school models. **Charter schools** frequently lack many benefits of public schools, including transportation, special educational services, second language programs, often visual and performance arts education, physical education, after-school programs, and the like.

Charters are positioned as competing with public schools, injecting that dose of competition and choice into the system despite evidence that such competition among charters and neighborhood schools does not really exist.[1] Charters and charter support organizations spend large sums of money advertising the schools to prospective parents. They also spend money seeking grants from philanthropic organizations to offset the lesser funding they receive from districts relative to the neighborhood schools. Charters depend heavily upon philanthropic funds. This means that they are less financially stable than neighborhood schools, while they are also heavily influenced by the agendas of the rich givers.

It is for this reason that the original mission of charters to develop independent and alternative school models has been largely replaced by the **venture philanthropy** agenda of creating homogenous models that are perceived as "scaleable" and "replicable" school models. Here again we see a neoliberal logic of applying private sector thinking to education. In this case, the goal of innovation and independence is supplanted by an emphasis on homogeneity and quantifiability in the interest of alleged high levels of control. Yet charters are often not held accountable for their often poor performance. What is more, charters have become a weapon in the arsenal of those neoliberals dedicated to destroying public schooling and replacing it with a privatized system. Chartering has been used across the United States to de-unionize schools and thereby eliminate the most potent opposition to privatization. The money that can be made by investors in privatizing public schools comes primarily from paying teachers less, hiring fewer teachers, getting rid of unions' rights to collectively bargain the terms and conditions of employment including wages, and getting rid of experienced, well-paid teachers, replacing them with inexperienced, low-paid teachers. It is no coincidence that teachers in charters have less experience and are paid less than neighborhood schoolteachers. It should also come as no surprise that charters do no better than their neighborhood counterparts when it comes to standardized test performance.[2] And despite the promises of cutting costs, administrative costs in charters are higher than in neighborhood schools.

Scholarship tax credits or what Kevin Welner has termed **neovouchers** work to use state tax credits to incentivize citizens to opt out of public schools and instead use private schools. These tax credits drain money and participation out of the public system while expanding privatization. This neoliberal strategy as well as the voucher strategy have been aggressively promoted by the Walton Family Foundation, the so-called philanthropic arm of the family that inherited the wealth of the late founder of the Wal-Mart Corporation. Neovouchers share the same problems as vouchers. Both of them encourage citizens to think of education as a private consumable service rather than a public good.

The neoliberal mantra of injecting market "competition and choice" into education has been embraced across the political spectrum. Concomitantly, a private sector model of "creative destruction" has been widely accepted in which schools should be "allowed to go out of business" and other schools should be opened to take their place. This **portfolio model** of school closures and openings is a system to foster contracting out the operation of schools, removing teachers' unions, and replacing administrations and teachers, weakening the job security of the teacher workforce.

For neoliberal proponents of these privatization schemes, the discipline of the market ought to be applied to the bureaucratic and inefficient public sector. In this view, the historical problems with public schools have to do with the very fact that the schools are public. This is a questionable conclusion, since the worst public schools have been subject to historical disinvestment and the best schools are public as well. Even accounting for the ways that urban and rural schools for the poor and working class have been historically shortchanged, the U.S. public school system still fares well in international comparisons on standardized test-based measures such as the OECD PISA. As David Berliner has long pointed out, there is a manufactured crisis of public school failure to justify privatization and defunding of the public schools most in need.

The crucial reality that the neoliberal "failure of public schooling" conceals is that public schooling is a public resource that is struggled over by different classes with different visions for what the schools should do. Moreover, this neoliberal idea of injecting market discipline into schools and onto teachers and administrators presumes that the basic problem facing schools is a lack of discipline and accountability. Such a view tends to isolate teacher performance from the broader context in which teachers teach. For example, while spectacularly successful public schools tend to enroll children from families with high levels of income and employment, extensive public and private social supports in communities, and related low rates of violence and crime in the area, spectacularly troubled public schools generally enroll children from families below poverty levels, with high rates of unemployment, a lack of public and private supports, and related high-violence crime in their communities. In place of the missing community supports arise illicit economies and social supports such as gangs and drugs. What is more, generational under-education and psychological depression is fostered in contexts of generational poverty and unemployment, as is a paucity of hope for a different future.

In other words, the challenges facing teachers in poor and working-class communities are not conditions that these teachers create. A new teacher entering a school quickly realizes that she did not de-industrialize the city center, outsource those jobs to the Pacific rim, systematically disinvest in quality public housing, racially segregate the city, and so on. The idea that individual teachers can compensate for these broader conditions if only they have the right teaching methods is ludicrous at best. Compounding the problem is that teachers are expected to delink learning from the social realities of students rather than making learning meaningful by relating it to the social context. Such meaningful learning can be the basis for reinterpreting the situation and acting collectively to change it in the best tradition of schooling for what John Dewey called **creative democracy**.

Profit Motives

Some of what is driving the neoliberal restructuring of public education is the quest for profit on behalf of educational for-profit corporations and investors. For example the multimillion-dollar for-profit management company sector (**educational management organizations,** or EMOs) is highly concentrated with fourteen large EMO corporations controlling 70 percent of schools being managed for profit.[3] For-profit EMOs manage schools mostly through contracts with charter school operators (94 percent) rather than through districts, indicating that the charter movement is fostering privatization. For-profit publishing companies, especially the largest such as NCS Pearson, McGraw-Hill, and ETS, publish both textbooks and tests, benefitting from and promoting the expansion of standardized testing and standardization of curriculum. Alongside strong-arming themselves into legislative processes at both the state and the national level, publishing companies are involved in numerous other educational for-profit ventures, from toy making to online services to special education remediation to teacher certification. There is a growing convergence between for-profit educational companies and for-profit media companies such as Bertelsmann and News Corporation, among others. For-profit educational companies and investors look at the $600 billion per year spent on public education as a huge source of wealth to be mined, and they compare the "education industry" to the defense, communications, and agricultural industries.

Ideological Motives

In addition to the profit motive driving the neoliberal privatization of education, there is a strong ideological component. Neoliberalism is an ideology that sees education not as a public good ideally serving a democratic society but as a private good primarily useful for preparing workers and consumers for the economy. In this view the social world is understood through radical individualism and a **social Darwinian** ethos. The individual should understand him- or herself foremost as an economic actor competing against others for scarce resources. Within this view, schooling should be oriented toward educational competition in preparation for economic competition, initially against others in the nation and then for competition against other nations. Knowledge in this view is framed as a consumable commodity that is efficiently or inefficiently delivered and consumed by students.

Many of the most powerful funders and promoters of neoliberal education come from the ranks of owners of large businesses. These people are true believers that because the private sector works for them, the private sector should be the model for the public sector and specifically public schooling. In reality, most of the other supporters of neoliberal education, despite not owning businesses, have learned to accept the framing and assumptions put forward by the funders and promoters. As media propaganda expands, this perspective grows more commonplace. As both political parties become more financially dependent on the campaign giving of rich donors, the legislative agenda favoring privatization—selling off public sector institutions to investors and advancing austerity measures while strong-arming the state to adopt more regressive and polarizing taxation—is likely to continue in its current direction of privatizing everything.

Neoliberal educational restructuring has no way of dealing with several crucial problems historically facing public schooling. Privatization such as chartering and vouchers do not challenge racial segregation and white flight in urban schooling. Instead they exacerbate segregation and naturalize an apartheid system of schooling and real estate markets. Public school reform instead ought to aim to dismantle racial, ethnic, and linguistic segregation as well as class segregation as part of a broader commitment to inclusive and equal democracy. Additionally, neoliberal reforms, including privatization but also high-stakes testing, standardization of curriculum, and union-bashing, offer nothing to challenge the legacy of radically unequal funding among public school districts. In fact, the neoliberal emphasis on "performance outcomes" not only narrows the curriculum and limits the intellectual inquiry characteristic of serious learning, but, when tied to funding as it has been in the past two decades, also punishes the poor and rewards the rich.

Title I funding that has historically been used to equalize funding has been reinvented to punish those schools and children not making standardized test score improvements. Neoliberalism's tendency for overemphasizing quantifiable outcomes fosters the anti-intellectualism of delinking knowledge from broader contexts, historical debates, and interpretations, while it also has a natural affinity for cultural conservative agendas that emphasize a common core of the "right" knowledge that students are to learn as dogma. This is illustrated by the for-profit company K12, Inc., which promotes a conservative version of history and literature while selling and expanding its meager product in charter schools and homeschooling by promising numerical measurement and the allure of technology in its online platform. The conservative cultural canon approach long championed by E. D. Hirsch and William Bennett, both investors in the company, undermines a view of learning as dialogical or related to questioning the production of knowledge. That is, this is a view of knowledge in which the ascribed social value on particular knowledge is mystified, and knowledge is treated as an object of reverence to be transmitted.

Conclusion

As neoliberal privatization and corporate models of restructuring expand, they create a new two-tiered educational system. The traditional public school system suffered from funding inequality, racial segregation, and anti-intellectual, anti-critical approaches to schooling—all problems that neoliberal school restructuring worsens. However, a successful struggle for integration, equality of resources, and critical intellectual approaches to schooling has been waged and continues to be pursued. Efforts to challenge the new two-tiered system cannot be restricted to schooling but must be linked to a broader social movement for democratic control and against corporate control over the economy, the political system, and the culture.

Suggested Further Reading

David Harvey. *A Brief History of Neoliberalism.* Oxford: Oxford University Press, 2007.

Perhaps the single most informative and influential book on neoliberalism.

Kenneth J. Saltman. *Collateral Damage: Corporatizing Public Schools—A Threat to Democracy.* Lanham, MD: Rowman & Littlefield, 2000.

An early analysis of the neoliberal restructuring of public schooling in the United States.

Robin Truth Goodman and Kenneth Saltman. *Strange Love Or How We Learn to Stop Worrying and Love the Market.* Lanham, MD: Rowman & Littlefield, 2002.

This book looks at the cultures of neoliberalism as they inform school curriculum, literature, and popular culture.

Kenneth J. Saltman. *The Edison Schools.* New York: Routledge, 2005.

A study of the largest for-profit educational management company in the United States (now called Edison Learning).

Kenneth J. Saltman. *Capitalizing on Disaster: Taking and Breaking Public Schools.* Boulder, CO: Paradigm, 2007.

This book addresses how natural and unnatural disasters have been used to justify neoliberal educational policy.

Kenneth J. Saltman. *The Gift of Education: Public Education and Venture Philanthropy.* New York: Palgrave Macmillan, 2010.

This book details the neoliberal agenda of the venture philanthropists such as the Gates, Broad, and Walton foundations and explains what is new and different from traditional philanthropy.

Kenneth J. Saltman. *The Failure of Corporate School Reform.* Boulder, CO: Paradigm, 2012.

This book contends that neoliberal educational restructuring has failed on its own terms of cost reductions and test score improvements as well as on terms of public democratic values. It relates the political economic dimensions of neoliberal education to the cultural politics of it and considers these in a global way. The book suggests rethinking educational values through the optic of a new common school movement. (For more on this topic, see Chapter Eleven in this volume.)

Henry A. Giroux. *Education and the Crisis of Public Values.* New York: Peter Lang, 2010.

This book offers a hard-hitting criticism of neoliberal educational policy from the vantage point of critical pedagogy.

Henry A. Giroux. *Against The Terror of Neoliberalism.* Boulder, CO: Paradigm, 2004.

This book explores the intersections of neoliberalism, militarism, and the security state since September 11.

Pauline Lipman. *The Political Economy of Urban Education.* New York: Routledge, 2010.

Lipman offers an insightful analysis of neoliberal educational restructuring focusing on Chicago.

Lois Weiner and Mary Compton (eds.). *The Global Assault on Teaching, Teachers, and Their Unions.* New York: Palgrave Macmillan, 2008.

David Hursh. *High Stakes Testing and the Decline of Teaching and Learning.* Lanham, MD: Rowman & Littlefield, 2008.

A criticism of the centrality of testing to neoliberal educational restructuring with a personal dimension.

Michael Apple. *Educating the Right Way.* New York: Routledge, 2001.

Apple maps the rightist movements fighting to influence public education including neoliberalism, neoconservatism, religious right, and authoritarian populist.

David Gabbard. *Knowledge and Power in the Global Economy,* 2nd ed. New York: Routledge, 2007.

An expansive edited collection, much of which addresses numerous dimensions of neoliberal education.

Questions for Discussion

1. What is neoliberalism as an economic doctrine, and how does this play out in public education?
2. What is neoliberalism as a cultural ideology, and how does this play out in public educational policy and practice?
3. Why do you think that the term "neoliberalism" is seldom used in mass media news and popular culture?

4. What are the dangers of treating public sector goods and services as if they are private?
5. What is unique about the public sphere, and why should public schooling be defended or strengthened in a democratic society?

Notes

1. See the abundant scholarship of David Berliner, who debunks the manufactured crisis and the myth of infusing market competition through privatization and high-stakes testing.

2. Kenneth J. Saltman, *The Failure of Corporate School Reform* (Boulder, CO: Paradigm, 2012).

3. See Gary Miron et al., "Profiles of For Profit and Non-Profit Educational Management Organizations, Thirteenth Annual Report 2010-2011," National Education Policy Center, January 2012; available at http://nepc.colorado.edu/publication/EMO-profiles-10-11.

Chapter Eight
The Politics of Gender in the Current Education Reforms

Since the early 1990s, market-based school reform has radically expanded in the United States. Gender has been utterly central to the expansion of neoliberal educational restructuring discussed in Chapter Seven. However, discussion of the centrality of gender has been largely absent from both scholarship and popular press coverage of educational reform. In the dominant narrative about education, there is a gendered subtext that has subtle yet powerful explanatory and symbolic power. This chapter lays out the material and symbolic war on women that is playing out through contemporary educational reform. The gendered subtext of educational reform underlies the unequal gendered labor force and the historical association of rationality with men and emotionality and experience with women. This chapter also includes a consideration of the academic response to gender inequality through the discourse of performativity.

The Material War on Women in Education

In the broader U.S. economy, women are paid 77 cents for each dollar a man earns while still largely doing a "second shift" of unpaid domestic labor. The disparity is even greater for women in racial and ethnic minorities. Women teaching at all levels of schooling from pre-kindergarten through university earn less than their male counterparts. What is more, women are overrepresented at the lower levels of education and underrepresented at the highest levels. The same pattern holds true for women working as teachers and as educational administrators. The higher one looks up the educational ladder, the fewer women there are in leadership roles and in teaching roles.

Furthermore, the educational disciplines are gendered in accordance with historical gendered discourses. Fields associated with "hard reason" such as philosophy or with hard science such as physics largely exclude women, while others associated with allegedly feminine caregiving and emotion such as nursing, social work, and early childhood education overrepresent women. Business follows a similarly gendered pattern, with women slotted into "soft" marketing and organizational behavior fields concerned with desires and relationships while men dominate the "hard" numbers arenas of finance. Dominant school reforms including privatization and standardized testing are based in the promise of greater inclusion into the workforce, yet these reformers offer no explanation for how exactly more testing and privatized ownership changes the historical gendered inequalities in the private sector.

The Symbolic War on Women in Education

In the market-based school reforms prevalent since the early 1990s, gendered metaphors have intersected with business and military metaphors. When corporate culture gets applied to schooling, neoliberal advocates of privatization employ metaphors that are linked by the invocation of masculine and corporeal discipline. Neoliberal educational restructuring calls for the hard discipline of the invisible hand of the market to impose competition and choice. In this framing of educational problems and solutions, the basic problem of teaching and learning stems from the failure of discipline on the part of individual teachers who need to instill and enforce the proper knowledge.

Major neoliberal educational reformers in the United States such as the Gates Foundation have sought to reduce a consideration of the quality of education to an evaluation of the quality of individual teachers and then to encourage business methods of disciplining the teacher workforce to coerce teachers to teach allegedly best one-size-fits-all methodologies. The federal troops-to-teachers program has steadily expanded and trains soldiers to be teachers and administrators, a program that promotes the idea that military discipline is what is needed in schools and that strong authoritative men are needed in a female and caregiving workforce. Educational leadership programs such as the Broad Superintendent Academy promote corporate and military leadership as the model of educational administration. This program both recruits future superintendents from corporations and the military and brings in speakers and instructors from these institutions. Implicit in such a program is an assumption that the hard, masculine discipline of market competition and a war-fighting ethos can enforce the "right" educational methods and the "right" knowledge.

Not just the particular programs such as the Broad Academy but the metaphors themselves further specific educational and social values. These values include an assumption of hierarchical and authoritarian social relationships in schools and society. The "good father" (even if he is a woman) must rule over those in his keeping and those in his keeping must submit to his authority. These values also include an assumption of knowledge as being imposed from above and aligned with authority rather than as being the result of dialogue and exchange. That is, democratic social relationships in schools and society and an ideal of equal and open exchange among participants is framed out of what schools should foster and practice—namely, efficient delivery of knowledge conceived of as units of commodity to be passively consumed by students. In this view, the omnipresent gaze of those in power, those who know but themselves cannot be seen, evaluate, assess, and hold "accountable" students and teachers through allegedly disinterested systems of control such as testing.

The Gendered Rationality/Experience Split as a Political Tactic in Education

The use of masculine metaphors in dominant reforms such as privatization and so-called data-driven instruction is interwoven with the promotion of allegedly neutral and objective and universally valuable curriculum, which can be quantifiably measured and tracked through standardized tests and standardized curriculum. The subjective experiences of students, not to mention teachers, are framed as an impediment to real learning in this view. Feelings, emotions, personal history, and individual reflection are treated as having nothing to do with what is taught and learned in schools. Individual and group experience is positioned as radically disconnected from learning and knowing. Real knowledge in the dominant framing is allegedly objective, not subjective; has to do with the mind, not the body; is about rationality, not feeling.

This framing repeats an ancient pattern in which masculinity is aligned with mind, rationality, agency, and universality, while femininity is aligned with body, emotion, passivity, and particularity. There are enormous political stakes in the repetition of this age-old framing. For example, in the Chicago Public Schools, 85 percent of students are below the poverty line and are nonwhite, predominantly African American and Latino/a. Students experience the ill effects of poverty such as homelessness and hunger, systematic disinvestment in communities including joblessness, and an absence of public and private infrastructure and supports. They also experience the psychological effects of this poverty and political abandonment not just as hopelessness, depression, and despair but also as a restricted sense of agency. The future possibilities that are most apparent to them are most prominently the church, the military, prison, or the gang. For the dominant view of schooling, these objective and subjective conditions of the student ought to be ignored and the teacher ought to enforce the allegedly objective and neutral knowledge on students through the most efficient methodologies.

However, the experience of the student matters in a number of ways. First, there is the question of why students should be motivated. Part of the reason there is such a high drop-out rate in urban schools is that the **official knowledge** taught in schools often has no relationship to what students experience as real life or see as real possibilities for the future. Second, if schools were to teach beginning with what students experience, then a meaningful and relevant pedagogy and curriculum could help students theorize, interpret, and act to change their own experiences and communities. In this critical view of education, experience is not the impediment to real learning or the basis for a **cultural deficit** but rather is the starting point for self and social transformation. That is not to say that experience can be trusted as transparent truth, that experience speaks for itself, or that all experience is authentic. Unfortunately, such false assumptions are frequently repeated whenever a teacher or administrator dismisses academic study or educational theory as opposed to the "lessons from the trenches" or the "real world" of the school. Experience matters, but it must always be interpreted. Part of what various academic traditions offer students is not just knowledge and facts but the tools to reconstruct and interpret their experiences in relation to broader social realities and struggles.

There is a conservative political tendency to reject student experience as irrelevant to real learning. Such a denial miseducates students to think of their own experiences as unrelated to the broader social totality. That is, it encourages students to think of what they experience as having no value and meaning in terms of the official knowledge of the school, a knowledge that allegedly does matter. A discounting of student experience effectively undermines student agency as students learn that what they know from experience should have no bearing on the institutions of power. Working-class and poor students and students of color learn that they should ignore or abandon what they know about hunger and excess, poverty and privilege, violence and security, injustice and justice, respect and disrespect, inclusion and exclusion, race and racism, cultural marginalization and valorization, rather than seeing these experiences as requiring investigation and seeing the curriculum as a place that can offer insights to reach a deeper understanding of such experiences.

Repeating a long colonial legacy of demanding cultural and linguistic assimilation to the group in power, contemporary educational reforms demand an abdication of individual and group difference and more importantly deny the intellectual tools to interpret the individual and social meanings and effects of these experiences. Within the dominant educational reform logic, cultural differences can be recognized only to identify an "achievement gap," but such a framing of the problem reaffirms the assumption that there is a universally valuable body of knowledge to be mastered and that individual experience has no relation to it.

Teacher education programs have been pushed in a similar direction in recent years with an emphasis on pairing teaching methods courses with so-called content knowledge (framing subjects apart from pedagogy or theory) courses and getting students into student teaching earlier than ever. This is based in the assumption that the experience in the school is inherently valuable and does not require theorization. There has been a tendency to devalue those foundations courses—such as sociology, philosophy, history, and politics of education—that give teaching candidates the tools for interpreting what they experience in schools and communities and for interpreting their own histories. This practicalism has to be understood as part of an effort for not just transforming education into something technical and bureaucratic as opposed to public and critical. It also has to be seen as playing on a long tradition of positioning women and girls as subordinate in educational institutions while rejecting serious consideration of the specific issues and problems facing women and girls, problems ranging from unequal work conditions to domestic and symbolic violence.

Inclusion and School to Work

Despite traditionally lagging behind boys in standardized tests, by the 2000s girls in school have come to equal and even surpass boys in traditional academic achievement defined by standardized tests. Girls even tend, in general, to do better than boys in academic disciplines, like math and the hard sciences where they were seen as lagging by the American Association of University Women (AAUW) a decade ago. It is for this reason perhaps that the educational reform efforts of the 2000s have focused more on race, ethnicity, and social class and not on gender. Yet these alleged gains in achievement are uneven when broken down by race, ethnicity, and social class. Working-class and poor girls, African American and Latina girls, and English-language learners do worse on the exams than do white girls.

The neoliberal restructuring in the last two decades has emphasized a view of schooling as being in the service of the economy and has misrepresented such service as being universally beneficial rather than as best serving those with the most power in that economy, namely those who own large corporations and industries. Neoliberals have promoted the purpose of education as being for individual economic mobility through the capitalist economy and for national economic competition in the global economy. Yet neoliberal educational restructuring has had little to say about the continuing gender inequality in the domestic and global labor force, whether the matter is women's lesser accessibility to "masculine" manual work, the gendered "glass ceiling" in management and professional work, the continued gendering of the caregiving labor force with the majority of new nurses being women, or the global preponderance of women in super-exploited positions as nannies and sweatshop workers in textile, electronics, and tech factories. In other words, there is a lot of rhetoric in the neoliberal educational reform that educational access translates to economic opportunity that doesn't accord with the realities of the gendered labor force.

If we take seriously the neoliberal concern with education for the economy but also take seriously democratic values for equality, justice, and fairness, then we are pressed to realize that gender inclusion in the educational system and workforce is not enough. To put it simply, equal gender access to labor exploitation domestically and globally is hardly a just vision for education. Instead, the organization of the workforce has to be transformed on both material and symbolic levels. Caregiving work needs to stop being valued as an extension of the domestic sphere, as marginal to the "real economy" or somehow de-skilled. Instead, it might behoove us to consider how common labor of such socially necessary and socially reproductive tasks could be geared toward the common good rather than the individualized benefit of owners. This raises the question of how democratic pedagogies might set the stage for a much more equal social arrangement by educating students in the values of shared work for shared benefit.

In academic studies of education and gender, certain perspectives have been prevalent. Feminist education analysis, led by scholars including Deborah Britzman and Elizabeth Ellsworth among others, draws on the insights of Lacanian psychoanalysis to investigate the ways that school tends to fix or close down meanings and identities. Such analysis reminds readers of the ways that meanings and identities are always in play, are only temporarily held in place. In this view, the role of the teacher is to defy the closure of signification and facilitate open interpretation. These insights are important in terms of valuing and interpreting the experiences and identities of students and teachers. However, some scholars coming from this perspective, such as Ellsworth and Charles Bingham, have a view of pedagogical authority that tends to align it with authoritarianism. That is, this perspective assumes that a teacher being explicit and directive about interpretations, even when justifying the view through reason, constitutes a violent closure of meaning. Such a perspective abdicates pedagogical authority while also missing how broader discourses inform interpretations. The view has little way of dealing with the systematic and institutional ways that meanings get made and the political economic interests and various ideologies that do pedagogical work in the absence of good teacher interventions. This understanding of teaching as withdrawn from normative political and ethical projects consequently offers little response to the neoliberal false promises of educational access for economic access.

Performativity

In the humanities, performativity theory is one widely used critical theory of gender. Scholars writing in education who have discussed performativity include Henry Giroux, Robin Truth Goodman, Stephen Ball, and Deborah Youdel. Contemporary theories of performativity offers a theory of identity formation most influenced by Judith Butler who draws on the philosophers Julia Kristeva,

Jacqueline Rose, Monique Wittig, Simone de Beauvoir, Joan Rivière, Gayle Rubin, Jacques Lacan, Michel Foucault, Friedrich Nietzsche, and Georg Hegel.

Performativity emphasizes that social interactions are performances and that identity is a performance rather than being essential, authentic, and pre-formed prior to actions. Butler's poststructuralist linguistically oriented version of performativity emphasizes that while we *are* nothing more than what we *do* (there is no actor before the act), what we do is animated by **discourse**—broader collections of ideas, meaning-making practices, institutional meanings, narratives, and legitimating practices. As a social construct, the self is "spoken" by discourse.

This view of the self differs from what is most commonly assumed about selves: that when they speak they unburden themselves of the authentic truth unique to that person. In the view of performativity, gender is something that is performed and gendered discourse is historically made. Every time we speak or act, we reproduce the norms of gender, but we also change it slightly by giving it a designation it did not have before we embodied it. For example, when fashion models dress up in feminine fashion, they both reproduce the norms of what it means to be a woman, but they also push the signifier of "woman" into a different context. The same goes for drag queens, who project an ideal of femininity that both glaringly reveals the content-meaning of femininity and discloses that there is no "real self," that femininity hides that what it designates is unstable and unfixed.

The signs and symbols of gender are taught and learned from the earliest age. Babies are draped in pink or blue, told they are "strong" or "pretty," and so on. Such meaning-making practices gender the subject. Gender is really a matter of process, something that is pedagogically achieved by gendering subjects in various institutions—the home, the school, the church, the media, the judicial system, the military, and so on. Because gender is a performance, at times its **social construction** and fragility become readily apparent. For example, the documentary film *Paris is Burning* features the transvestite balls in New York City in the 1980s, where men and transsexuals perform extremely feminine displays, sometimes invoking famous female celebrities. There are also gay men dressed up as members of the military, as kids in school, as businessmen, or even as "normal." The film raises the question of whether these men are more authentically female than women by virtue of their seamless performances of femininity. It also questions whether, when these drag queens dress as men, they move the signifier "men" toward a slightly different content. Butler, who comments on the film, challenges the alignment of gender with biological sex, suggesting that biological sex itself is only made meaningful through gender.

This perspective differs from the common mapping of gender to biological reproductive capacity. The body and its organs are only meaningful through historically constituted relations of difference and distinction. The question arises of which sex differences become the ones that matter in making cultural categories, and why, as opposed to say other arbitrary physical or nonphysical patterns of difference. In this way, as Stuart Hall has pointed out, gender as a social construction shares a lot with race as a social construction. There is no truth of gender or race that can be ultimately grounded in biological difference or particular symbols. Butler's performativity offers a strong sense of individual agency (the sense of the capacity to act on and shape the social and symbolic world); while individuals repeat the already existing signs of gender, they also re-signify them—that is, they oftentimes rework these meanings. Gender as a discursive construct means that while there is no getting outside of gender, like all language there are always creative possibilities in what sorts of meanings individuals can make.

Conclusion

Considered as a performance, identity intersects with many contemporary school issues and problems, from gender and sexed bullying and sexual education to how subject matter such as history, English, social studies, and science might be approached. There are high stakes in how teachers and cultural workers address questions of gender inside and outside of schools. Cultural categories are taught and learned and people are produced as particular kinds of gendered and racial subjects. It takes a tremendous amount of pedagogical work to maintain and reproduce this existing gender hierarchy, and it also takes a tremendous amount of denial of the pedagogical production of subjectivity and naturalization of these fictive categories. An important critical pedagogical task is to undo the limiting, narrow versions of gender and race, to "read them as texts," to call into question their naturalness and inevitability, to investigate the ways that gender and race practices and meanings are linked to broader interests, power relations, and institutional formations, and to imagine ways of transforming them. Such investigation into the ways that gender is linked to power relations and institutions can form the basis for pedagogical practices, counterpedagogies, and social movements to create new and more egalitarian and emancipatory institutions and social arrangements.

Suggested Further Reading

Judith Butler. *Gender Trouble.* New York: Routledge, 1991.
The most significant book on gender performativity. It suggests that, rather than understanding gender as a social construction that is a function of a foundational biological sex, sex is a discursive construct and the effect of gender performance.

Judith Butler. *Undoing Gender.* New York: Routledge, 2004.
A collection of essays after *Gender Trouble* on gender and performance.

Michel Foucault. *History of Sexuality, Vol. I.* New York: Vintage, 1980.
A groundbreaking work establishing the discursive construction of sex, explaining the confessional technology of power, and discussing the theory of biopolitics.

Robin Truth Goodman. *World Class Women.* New York: Routledge, 2004.
An important engagement with feminist pedagogy and literary studies.

Deborah Britzman. *Lost Subjects, Contested Objects.* Albany: SUNY Press, 1998.
A Lacanian psychoanalytic approach to teaching.

Deborah Britzman. *Practice Makes Practice.* Albany: SUNY Press, 2003.

Elizabeth Ellsworth. *Teaching Positions.* New York: Teachers College Press, 1998.
A Lacanian psychoanalytic approach to the "impossibility" of teaching.

Questions for Discussion

1. How is it that women continue to earn less than men in the workforce?
2. What is meant by a symbolic war on women?
3. How do the dominant educational reforms fail to address gender inequality?
4. How is the performativity theory of gender different from other more common conceptions of gender?
5. What would a critical pedagogical approach to gender require, and how is that different from the dominant educational trends?

Chapter Nine
The Politics of Globalization and Education

This chapter discusses how the neoliberal educational restructuring facing the United States is a global phenomenon with high stakes for citizens everywhere. The stage is being set for a corporate takeover of public education on a global scale.

Global Corporate Schooling

In rich nations, corporations, governments, think tanks, and consultants have succeeded in privatizing, deregulating, and corporatizing public education to an unprecedented extent. Supranational organizations such as the International Monetary Fund, World Bank, and World Trade Organization promote a for-profit model of schooling in poor countries, pushing educational development away from public school creation and toward privatization. There are vast material and ideological struggles at play in what corporations see as a multibillion-dollar industry ripe for the taking.

One of the most high-profile cases of corporations aiming to build and dominate a future global market in for-profit school services is that of **Christopher Whittle** who created Avenues, an elite private school in the United States. Whittle plans to leverage the brand to sell knock-off for-profit online learning in poor nations. Whittle, likening his education business to selling luggage in airports, plans for a concentrated global market in education modeled on the massive for-profit educational management industry in the United States.[1] Another corporation staking its claims on a global education market is the conglomerate Knowledge Universe, created by junk bond felon **Michael Milken** who bought up for-profit education companies, including online cyberschool **K12, Inc.**, to become the United States' largest **educational management organization** (EMO) while expanding for-profit higher education in Singapore.[2] Multinational corporations such as News Corp and Microsoft also look to aggressively expand for-profit education initiatives, joining the likes of publishing giants such as **Pearson NCS** and McGraw-Hill. Corporate consultants such as **McKinsey Consultants** globetrot to implement private sector approaches to educational restructuring in the United Kingdom, United States, and around the world. Policy promotion and media spectacle merge as supranational organizations, corporations, and think tanks work to prevent the development of universal, free public education in poorer nations such as India, where public education is desperately needed.

Public education that is universally available and free is necessary for literacy and critical literacy for full political participation, for technological development, for struggles for national independence from rich nations and autonomy—in short to create the conditions for a free, just, and prosperous society. The development of privatized education means that those with more wealth benefit while those with the least are punished and everyone is beholden to spend precious wealth on what could be a public service. Meanwhile, celebrities, journalists, politicians, and philanthropists join nongovernmental organizations (NGOs) and corporate media in presenting public schooling as a failure or an impossibility and frame the rich as being the only ones who can save the poor with for-profit schooling.

Supranational Organizations

Several powerful U.S.-dominated international organizations have been working toward simultaneously undermining public educational development in poor countries and promoting for-profit schooling in those places. The World Trade Organization (WTO) represents multinational corporations and has put in place trade rules for nations in line with neoliberal economic views, especially replacing nations' regulation of trade with corporate regulation of trade. Such corporate regulation of trade allows private service providers to compete in markets and does not protect industry in poorer economies. Most significantly, such corporate regulation on trade makes no distinction between public non-profit and private for-profit educational endeavors. The General Agreement on Trade in Services (GATS) provision of the WTO treats all educational services, whether public or private, as if they were private and consequently sets the stage for all public education systems to be subject to market competition against for-profit companies.

The implications of this policy are enormous. It eradicates the very idea of schooling as a free, universal good directed toward serving the public interest and creating engaged citizens. Instead, schooling in this policy can only be a business aiming to maximize profit and preparing students for assimilation into private economic endeavors. A nation in North America or Europe would be required under GATS to submit to market competition from foreign education companies, which could be staffed with teachers from poor countries and paid according to home country pay scale. GATS sets the stage for super-exploited international teacher work. It also sets the stage for large multinational companies from the rich countries to privatize public education in poor countries and, by homogenizing content and massifying sales and production, to impose standardized curricula and pedagogical approaches that have the most lucrative economies of scale. The arrangement undermines local autonomy while at the same time creating conditions for public funding to be skimmed out of educational processes in the form of profit. As with all of the "free trade" infrastructure imposed by the WTO, the business interests from the richer nations stand to benefit most economically by forcing poorer countries to open borders for the dumping of cheap product or service, undermining the local infrastructures. Once the local infrastructures are dismantled, typically the foreign company raises prices.

IMF/World Bank

At the end of World War II the Allies established the World Bank and International Monetary Fund (IMF) during the Bretton Woods Agreement. These institutions were intended to help rebuild nations devastated by the war, but they also sought to promote a particular form of development favored by the United States in which capitalist economics would be merged with liberal democratic electoral politics. Such development was positioned against the Soviet alternative of a one-party state and planned, centralized economy. Yet the U.S. model functioned as well to assure governmental structures that would serve U.S. power elites by deterring the development of more direct forms of political democracy and participatory forms of economics. By the 1980s the World Bank and IMF shifted their emphasis to promote the so-called Washington consensus of neoliberalism. The Washington consensus involved privatization, market deregulation, and the allowance of foreign direct investment.

The World Bank and IMF expanded lending during the 1980s and 1990s. Such lending was responsible for vastly expanding third world debt servitude. With the wave of decolonization sweeping Africa in the 1960s, former colonies were left desperate for money. The World Bank and IMF loaned new nations money at high interest rates and with so-called structural adjustment loan conditions. These conditions required nations to privatize and sell off national infrastructure while opening barriers to imports and allowing foreign companies access to the national markets. The implications of these policies were dire for economies, citizens, and public institutions, including public schooling.

As nations borrowed money they became more and more indebted to foreign banks, and the gross domestic product was spent not on hospitals, schools, roads, and other public infrastructure but on servicing high-interest debt. As the trade barriers were lowered, rich companies arrived and dumped products at low costs to wipe out the indigenous industries. Once the indigenous industry was gone, they jacked up the prices on their inferior goods.

A good example of this is in Jamaica, where cheap imports of powdered milk decimated the Jamaican fresh milk industry. Once the last dairy cows were turned into hamburger, the price of powdered imported milk was raised. With its economy in ruins from structural adjustment, Jamaica began competing to attract low-paid jobs from global corporations. For example, Jamaica opened the Kingston and Montego Bay Tax Free Zones, which paid workers less than a dollar an hour to make underwear, do telemarketing, and edit academic textbooks for the U.S. market. The businesses operating in these Tax Free Zones paid no taxes, so that the Jamaican schools, roads, and hospitals received no money from these operations. In short, the structural adjustment policies were a recipe for worsening debt, gutted-out public goods and services such as schools, and lowered standards of living in the places that were desperate enough to borrow under these conditions.

Now the World Bank's educational "development" projects promote not the development of free, universally available, and public schooling but rather the development of privatized, for-profit, and fee-for-service forms of schooling. The World Bank has come under the sway of British education scholar **James**

Tooley who contends that only if poor students are forced to pay for school will they have a "stake" in it. He explains in his book *The Beautiful Tree* that he imagines the schools in poor nations in the future being modeled on the American fast-food industry.[3] Unfortunately, Tooley and the World Bank have abandoned the use of its financial power and influence to induce and financially support nations to expand public educational services, opting instead to promote privatization.

Together these international NGOs, nationally based humanitarian organizations such as **USAID**, and corporate philanthropists such as the Gates Foundation and the Clinton Global Initiative form what some international comparative education scholars such as Susan Robertson and Stephen Ball refer to as a shifted terrain of **global governance** over education. That is, these organizations, despite being controlled by a small number of political and fiscal elites, are able to determine educational policy for the vast majority of citizens. This is a decidedly anti-democratic arrangement.

In the case of the corporate philanthropies, there is an unfair and anti-democratic economic dimension to the giving away of educational governance. Corporate philanthropies such as the Gates, Walton, Broad, and Pearson foundations are only made possible by public tax subsidies in which the public forgoes tax revenue, allowing rich donors and corporations to avoid paying taxes on income. These donors then put that money into their own foundations, allowing them to steer, direct, and influence educational policy. In some cases the influence has been truly massive, such as the Gates Foundation's ability to expand charter schooling and corporate "turnaround" strategies for school reform. In effect, the public subsidizes the abdication of public control over public goods and services such as schooling. Then such subsidized de-democratization is represented in for-profit media venues as generosity, care, and goodwill on the part of the richest citizens rather than as the hijacking of the public sector.

USAID

Nationally based humanitarian organizations such as the United States Agency for International Development (USAID) has been involved with so-called **democracy promotion** projects around the world that often involve projecting U.S. power and influence over the political process. In its educational development activities,

USAID frames its work through the lens of economic development and expanding inclusion into capitalism. USAID is led by a former Gates Foundation leader and shares with Gates the emphasis on performance-based outcomes, measurability of activities, and withdrawal of support from those educational projects that are difficult to numerically measure for efficacy. The Gates Foundation has been a major proponent of public school privatization in the form of charter school expansion and corporate models of educational leadership. USAID shares with right-wing **Hoover Institution** fellow **Erik Hanushek** the idea that education translates to economic benefits for everyone. In this view, more years of education guarantee more individual income. This is a highly simplistic perspective about the relationship between education and personal financial success (discussed earlier in Chapter Two). It cannot account for the many people who have been the victims of neoliberal globalization such as the unemployed, university-educated Americans whose jobs went overseas due to deregulation, or the engineers with PhDs driving taxis all over India. The ideological agenda equating schooling with raised incomes frames public education as a private consumable commodity and thereby sets the stage for privatizing it—an agenda central to the Hoover Institution's education work.

Conclusion

Ideally public education imagines individual opportunity as being inextricably linked to the formation of egalitarian social relations and the response to public problems. The most pressing problems facing the global public include ecological crisis, poverty, radical inequalities in wealth and income, resource wars, political authoritarianism, militarism, and cultural domination. By promoting individualized forms of subjectivity, global corporate schooling cannot adequately address these public crises and in fact it exacerbates them by undermining the critical intellectual tools for teachers and students to publicly confront these problems. As the public cedes control over schooling to the private sector, the public roles of schooling are replaced by corporate training, and the range of thinking is restricted to that which falls within the ideological frames of the pursuit of profit. The vision for public democratic education on a global scale must not only burst the national frame but offer an alternative to the congealing of the new corporate system. The time is ripe for a new global vision for public education.

Suggested Further Reading

Stephen Ball. *Global Education Inc.* New York: Routledge, 2012.

A recent mapping of the powerful global players in the corporatization of education.

Kenneth Saltman. *Capitalizing on Disaster: Taking and Breaking Public Schools.* Boulder, CO: Paradigm, 2007.

Provides a view of corporatization projects in nations including the United States, Iraq, Afghanistan, Haiti, and Nicaragua drawing on critical globalization studies.

Joel Spring. *Globalization of Education.* New York: Routledge, 2008.

Spring's book offers an introductory overview that is unique in its attention to religious schooling.

Susan Robertson and Roger Dale's website and journal *Globalisation, Education, and Societies.*

This is one of most comprehensive and valuable resources on globalization and education coming largely from a critical perspective.

Fazal Rizvi and Bob Lingard. *Globalizing Education Policy.* New York: Routledge, 2009.

William I. Robinson (ed.). *Critical Globalization Studies.* New York: Routledge, 2004.

Robinson's collection provides a variety of valuable theoretical chapters on a range of international issues focused on questions of power struggles and politics.

Hugh Lauder et al. *Education, Globalization, and Social Change.* Oxford: Oxford University Press, 2006.

Questions for Discussion

1. What are the global forces involved in reshaping education?
2. How do the global struggles over educational futures relate to what has been discussed in other chapters about the U.S. context?
3. What is at stake politically and ethically in the increasingly private control over public schooling around the world as typified by the WTO's GATS or Christopher Whittle's vision of a concentrated massive education industry that spans the planet?

4. Why do you think nonstate and nongovernmental institutions, which are not-for-profit, often accept the business framing of the problems and solutions for public schooling in rich and poor countries?

Notes

1. Christopher Whittle, talk at AEI, "The Rise of Global Schooling," December 7, 2009, available at http://www.aei.org/event/100146.

2. Robin Truth Goodman and Kenneth J. Saltman, *Strange Love or How We Learn to Stop Worrying and Love the Marke*t (Lanham, MD: Rowman & Littlefield, 2002).

3. James Tooley, *The Beautiful Tree: A Personal Journey Into How the World's Poorest People Are Educating Themselves* (New York: CATO, 2009).

Chapter Ten
The Politics of the Status Quo or a New Common School Movement?

This chapter, which is adapted from Kenneth J. Saltman, *The Failure of Corporate School Reform*, aims to appropriate elements from the original common school movement along with elements from the new discourse on the commons to consider how different forms of public and private control over schooling produce the common or enclose it. It suggests strengthening public schooling by reinventing the traditional common school movement in order to create the conditions for collective forms of living and working throughout society. In doing so, it pushes the critical education perspective toward expanding its focus from schooling for political engagement and cultural interpretation toward centrally focusing as well on schooling for egalitarian forms of economic activity.

U.S. public schooling developed from the **common school** movement of the nineteenth century led in Massachusetts by reformer **Horace Mann**. While Mann's project included the virtues of expanding universal and secular public education and expanding civic education for civic participation, it also aimed for the problematic aspirations of cultural assimilation and imposition of dominant cultural values and vocational preparation.

Recent literature in the humanities and social sciences on the commons offers a way of thinking about the politics of education in terms of the expansion or enclosure of the common labor of the teacher, student, administrator, the common land of the school building, and the common material resources for teaching and learning. Moreover the economy is increasingly organized around the central aspects of education—namely, knowledge-making and the pedagogical work that goes into the making of selves. That is, according to a number of scholars associated with the **autonomist** movement, contemporary advanced capitalism has, at its core, knowledge-making and subjectivity-producing activity.

As previous chapters have discussed, the current educational reform policies coming from both Democrats and Republicans are oriented around an assumption that schooling should be primarily for assimilation of the individual into the existing arrangement of work in a capitalist economy. This view makes a number of assumptions about the relationship between knowledge and the economy that are questionable and challenged by other perspectives, including the liberal view of Horace Mann and the original common school movement and the more radically democratic view of the new scholarship on the commons.

The Original Common School Movement

The U.S. public school system has its origins in the common school movement spearheaded first in Massachusetts by Horace Mann in the early nineteenth century. The movement eventually spread throughout the United States. Mann emphasized the need for an educated public for a functioning democracy, a system of publicly financed schools, that schools should be composed of children of different backgrounds, that education should be nonsectarian, that students should be taught by professionally trained teachers, and that the educational disciplines and methods should express the values of a free society. The common school movement was promoted as a means of political inclusion, workforce preparation, and individual character-building aiming to bring together children of different classes and provide a common learning experience. The common school movement sought to increase and to improve the provision of educational resources including the quality of schools, increased duration of schooling to the age of sixteen, better pay for the mostly female teacher workforce, and a broader curriculum.

While many aspects of public schooling have been struggled over since the common school movement, including racial segregation and integration, the question of secular versus religious-based moral instruction, the politics of the curriculum, and the role of public schools in workforce preparation, neoliberal privatization in the last twenty years has in many respects undone many socially valuable aspects of the legacy of the common school movement. The aspirations for a common educational experience, the commitment to nonsectarian schooling, and the value of educated citizenry for public participation are collateral damage in the privatization trend. Voucher schemes, homeschooling, and scholarship tax credits have contributed to an effort by especially the **Christian Right** to capture public resources to pay for religious education. In this case we witness the merger of **market fundamentalism** in the service of expanding religious forms of fundamentalism. In both cases faith—faith in markets or faith in a religion—trumps critical forms of reason and civic discourse while submission to authority is elevated over dissent and disagreement central to democratic debate.

The neoliberal emphasis on schooling for work and consumption has dramatically undermined the central value on promoting democratic citizens imbued with the knowledge and dispositions for self-governance. The relentless push for charter schooling has resegregated public schools. **Magnet schools** were transformed as well during the Reagan presidency from being an effort in racial integration and equity into being seen as a "market" in schools. The universal and equal provision of education that is publicly funded has been damaged severely by the centrality of the metaphors of competition and consumer choice. In addition to transforming schooling into something that is more class-stratified, neoliberal privatization redefines schooling into an individualized responsibility, undermining the sense of shared value for the benefit of others.

Corporate school reform or neoliberal educational restructuring represents hopelessness for the future and an assumption that unlimited capitalist growth is the only alternative. That is, corporate school reform not only actively contributes to the reproduction of economic exploitation, political marginalization, and the crushing of imagination as all social and individual values are reduced to market concerns; it also contributes to planetary destruction, which makes life on the planet a kind of terminal illness while waiting out the imminent cascade of ecological collapse and human disaster in responding to it. As a number of scholars have suggested, capitalism and its imperative for unlimited growth of consumption is a waste production system, despoiling not only the planet but rendering wasted lives and disposable populations.[1] But corporate school reform installs and extends a culture of control that is at odds with freedom understood as collectively enacted aspirations. As well, the economic promises of corporate school reform are false promises. The promise of corporate school reform toward the end of workforce preparation and university enrollment has no way of dealing with the global race to the bottom for cheap, precarious labor. Corporate school reform asks citizens to have faith in corporations for their future economic well-being. Such faith is profoundly misplaced not only because the institutional interests of corporations aim primarily (by law) for profit first but also because gains in labor conditions such as the end of child labor, the creation of the weekend, the eight-hour workday, and benefits were the result not of the beneficence of corporations but of social movements. Indeed, as the low-paid Jamaican proofreaders of academic textbooks illustrate, global corporate governance infrastructure that deregulates capital and labor and defunds the public sector creates the conditions for a super-exploited highly educated labor force. Preventing that requires either revitalized labor movement, social democratic state intervention, or, as Richard Wolff has argued, the collectivization of industries such that workers and managers become the same people.[2]

Corporate School Reform as an Enclosure of the Commons

Corporate school reform or neoliberal educational restructuring represents not merely better or worse school reform approaches—adjusting pedagogical methods, tweaking the curriculum, and so on. It is also crucially about redistributed control over social life, and as such is part of a much broader trend. It represents a capitalist **enclosure** of the commons—that is the violent taking of "the shared substance of our social being."[3] As philosopher **Slavoj Zizek** points out, there are four crucial enclosures of the commons at present:

> *the commons of culture*, the immediately socialized forms of "cognitive capital", primarily language, our means of communication and education, but also the shared infrastructure of public transport, electricity, the postal system, and so on;
> *the commons of external nature*, threatened by pollution and exploitation (from oil to rain forests and the natural habitat itself);
> *the commons of internal nature* (the biogenetic inheritance of humanity); with new biogenetic technology, the creation of a New Man [sic] in the literal sense of changing human nature becomes a realistic prospect.[4]

A fourth enclosure of the commons involves the de facto apartheid situation of new "walls and slums" that physically enclose people, separating the Excluded from the Included. These four enclosures of the commons are being struggled over and the stakes in the struggle are, for Zizek, the very survival of the species and the planet itself. Capitalist enclosure of the natural commons produces ecological catastrophe. Capitalist enclosure of the knowledge commons makes ideas into private property rather than freely shared and exchanged knowledge of use and potential universal benefit. Capitalist enclosure transforms the biological information that is the stuff of life into property, setting the stage for new forms of bio-slavery and profit-based control.

Corporate school reform colludes with and deepens these enclosures of the commons. It makes knowledge into a commodity rather than letting it be shared and freely exchanged. It presents a natural world pillaged for private ownership rather than stewarded for public care. It privatizes the process of maturation and socialization, making human development into business and children into product. Finally, the lower tier of privatized public schooling expands repression in the form of "new walls and slums"—that is the expansion of repressive schooling targeting the poor and particularly urban nonwhite youth with zero-tolerance policies, heavy police presence and security apparatus in schools, rigid pedagogies oriented around bodily control, and so on.

The most significant aspect of corporate school reform involves privatizing the public schools. In an economic sense, privatization involves enclosing commonly held wealth, assets, and land. Value is produced by collective labor in any enterprise. But capitalism individualizes the profits from collective labor. As David Harvey points out, the commons as a form of collective laboring must ground collective rather than individualized property rights and result in collective control over the production process.[5] Public schools are not simply commonly held property but the collective labor of teachers, administrators, and staff as well. As Harvey explains,

> the collective laboring that is now productive of value must ground collective, not individual, property rights. Value, socially necessary labor time, is the capitalist common, and it is represented by money, the universal equivalency by which common wealth is measured. The common is not, therefore, something extant once upon a time that has since been lost, but something that, like the urban commons, is continuously being produced. The problem is that it is just as continuously being enclosed and appropriated by capital in its commodified and monetary form.[6]

Corporate school reform encloses and appropriates for capital the collective *labor* of teachers, administrators, staff, and students. And it does so by using public financing for privatizing public schooling.

In fact, as real estate schemes by charters and the vast array of contracting deals exemplify, corporate school reform also encloses the collective *property* of the public school. In some cases the actual public school building is given to a private entity such as a charter school. More frequently, the contracting arrangements that districts make with for-profit firms result in the extraction of surplus wealth, most often by decreasing teacher pay and skimming off profit by contractors. For Harvey, the problem of the commons is that unregulated individualized capital accumulation threatens to destroy the laborer and the land—the two most basic common property resources. The extent of these destructions to the common property resources of the public schools includes, for example, how unregulated individualized capital accumulation destroys teacher labor by transforming work from being intellectual, civically engaged, dialogic fostering of curiosity, questioning, and dissent into an anti-intellectual, depoliticized, dogmatic, transmissional, curiosity-deadening, and creativity-stifling process.

Corporate school reform destroys not only the public and civic dimensions of schooling but also the economic productive force of it. Unregulated individualized capital accumulation also destroys the labor of the student and the economic productiveness of the student's future economic labor. The overemphasis on standardized testing and curriculum devalues the teacher's engagement with the specific context and experience of the student and in doing so makes it impossible for the act of teaching to produce the kind of subject that would engage in collective creative production. Corporate school reform steals the student's relationship to both creative activity and to time.

The promise of corporate school reform for its proponents is that it increases the efficiency of the teacher-laborer through the enforcement of discipline (tighter controls over time, subject matter, and pedagogical methods) and that such efficiency increases the delivery of knowledge to the student-consumer, increasing, in turn, the potential economic efficiency of the future student-worker. The promise is false at every point. For example, chartering has been captured by a corporate logic and aims to replicate and scale up the most efficient delivery models, extend the teacher day, pay teachers less, burn teachers out, and turn over the teacher workforce. All of these are proven effects of chartering, and there is no doubt that these are good means of maximizing short-term profit for management companies and other contractors.

The problem is not only, as a liberal like Darling-Hammond emphasizes, that these destructive reforms are bad for test-based student achievement.[7] More significantly, these are means of worsening the creative, intellectual, curiosity-fostering, and critically engaged qualities of teaching and also worsening the future productive force of the students' labor.[8] But controlled, rigid, anti-critical teaching results not in subjects with a greater capacity for economic productivity, but the opposite. If the goal is to produce docile, disciplined, low-skill workers or marginalized people who are excluded from the economy altogether, then these corporate school reforms are right on target. However, ethics and politics aside, this is shortsighted as an economic strategy if, as the corporate school reformers allege, the aim of public schooling is to produce future high-tech workers with knowledge of math and science and the creativity to create new projects and create new value.

The dominant justification for corporate school reform is for the United States to develop its labor capacity in the tech arena in order to win global economic competition. Usually, proponents of the dominant justification call for encouraging students to develop their capacities for entrepreneurialism. It is difficult to see how eroding the capacity of teacher labor to inspire vigorous, creative thinking and intellectual curiosity could contribute to such a capitalist goal. Even on its own (bad) terms, corporate school reform fails. Enclosure of the public school through privatization does create short-term profit, but it destroys the labor and resources of the public school. As I have argued and illustrated in *Capitalizing on Disaster*, such pillaging of public services has become a means for the acquisition of short-term profit by ruling-class people while destroying long-term value for everyone else.

Lois Weiner argues that despite the rhetoric of "excellence promotion" corporate school reforms are designed to de-skill and de-professionalize teachers and produce a low-paid, low-skilled future workforce for their students (educated to the eighth grade).[9] Weiner's attention to how this plays out in the documents and practices of global economic organizations such as the World Bank and International Monetary Fund are confirmed in the United States in the form, for example, of the 21st Century Skills initiative as well as the report Tough Choices for Tough Times—policy reports that aim to promote a business perspective for public schooling. There is official rhetoric, for example, coming from the Gates Foundation and the U.S. Department of Education, that individual economic opportunity will come from increasing high school and graduation rates.[10] Yet these claims invert cause and effect by suggesting that the education level of the individual creates the job opportunity instead of recognizing that the high levels of low-pay, low-skill unemployment are structurally part of the economy.[11]

Put differently, we must ask whether high levels of education create employment. Evidence suggests that political maneuvering and economic development activities to lure professional jobs to states and municipalities are more about stealing jobs from other states and locales than it is about job creation.[12] There is a domestic race to the bottom for jobs in which states compete to see who can offer the best tax breaks to businesses. And while education is marketed as providing professional-class jobs, the United States continues to lose those jobs to nations with cheaper labor costs but high education levels; legal jobs, accounting jobs, and IT jobs going from the United States to India and Singapore are the obvious examples. Without protections, such labor disappears in the global race to the bottom.

Another neoliberal argument for education for economic development (found for example in the *New York Times* columns of Thomas L. Friedman) suggests that students need to be made into entrepreneurs so that they can add value to the corporate workplace. In this absurd tale, entrepreneurship is primarily a matter of schooling rather than a matter of capital outlay. This argument relies on the narrow case of young innovators developing Facebook apps that net advertising revenue. Such thinking can be found in Linda Darling-Hammond's *The Flat World and Education* where she affirms Friedman's assumptions by claiming that schools need to be improved because the workers of tomorrow will be doing jobs that do not yet exist. For Friedman, Darling-Hammond, the majority of the educational establishment, and popular discourse, education sets the stage for global economic capitalist competition. In these ways of thinking about education, reform aims toward future *collective labor* to be directed toward *individualized gains.*

Distinguishing between Public and Private Control in Education

If we consider corporate school reform in terms of the recent literature on the commons, we can ask the question of how it helps us formulate a response to the problems posed by public school privatization in terms of economic control, political control, and cultural control. The issue at stake here is not whether privatization threatens critical, public, and democratic forms of education. We begin with assuming that as a given. Rather the question is this: *How do critical forms of education create the conditions for collective labor toward collective benefit, and how do private forms of education create the conditions for collective labor toward private benefit?*

Part of what is at stake in the privatization of schools is the diminishment of the public sphere. We should recognize that there are at least four clear ways that those committed to democratic education must understand how public control differs from private control.

1. Public versus private ownership and control: For-profit education companies are able to skim public tax money, otherwise reinvested in educational services, and shunt it to investor profits. These profits take concrete form as the limousines, jet airplanes, and mansions that public tax money provides to rich investors. These profits also take symbolic form as they are used to hire public relations firms to influence parents, communities, and other investors to have faith in the company. This is a parasitical financial relationship that results in the management of the schools in ways that will maximize the potential profit for investors while cutting costs. This has tended to result in anti-unionism, the reduction of education to the most measurable and replicable forms, assaults on teacher autonomy, and so on. Anti-unionism results not just in worsened work conditions, pay, and benefits for teachers but lower quality in the form of higher teacher turnover and a less experienced teacher workforce. Indeed, the nations that outscore the United States in standardized test performance have both strong teachers unions and a strong collaboration between unions and administrators. There is no evidence that the draining of public wealth and its siphoning to capitalists has improved public education or that it is required for the improvement of public education. Moreover, such a redistribution over economic control shifts the collective control over the processes of teaching and learning to the owner or private manager of the privatized educational approach. It captures such educational labor and channels it toward profit-making for owners in the short term and future exploitable capitalist labor relations in the long term.
2. Public versus private cultural politics: Privatization affects the politics of the curriculum. A for-profit company and a nonprofit dependent on a private venture philanthropy cannot have a critical curriculum that makes central, for example, the ways that privatization threatens democratic values and ideals. While most public schools do not have wide-ranging critical curricula, the crucial issue is that some do, and most could. This is a matter of public struggle. Privatization forecloses such struggle by shifting control to private hands and prohibiting pedagogies that are at odds with institutional and structural interests. Democratic society requires citizens capable of debate, deliberation, dissent, and intellectual engagement. Privatization

fosters anti-democratic instrumental and transmission-oriented approaches to pedagogy. The privatization of mass media represents an important parallel to the privatization of public schooling with regard to cultural politics. For-profit media disallows representations and questioning that runs counter to the institutional interests.[13] For example, there was no corporate media news coverage of the public giveaway of the digital band spectrum to media conglomerates. Likewise, corporate media never covers the possibilities of alternative economic systems that are more egalitarian or more directly democratic. With corporate school reform, the overemphasis on standards and standardization, testing, and accountability replicates a corporate logic in which measurable task performance and submission to authority become central. Intellectual curiosity, investigation, teacher autonomy, and critical pedagogy, not to mention critical theory, have no place in this view. **Critical** in this context means not merely problem-solving skills but the skills and dispositions for criticizing how particular claims to truth secure particular forms of authority. Democratic forms of education enable critical forms of agency, fostering political interpretation that can form the basis for collective social action. Critical curriculum and school models could provide the means for theorizing and acting to challenge the very labor exploitation to which schools such as these prepare students to submit.

3. Public versus private forms of publicity and privacy, including secrecy and transparency: Private companies are able to keep much of what they do secret. EMOs and charter schools that straddle the line between public and private selectively reveal financial and performance data that would further their capacity to lure investors. Such manipulation is endemic to privatization schemes. Such secrecy represents a tactic on the part of privatizers to disallow collective control over school financing and budgets. The secrecy of privatization prevents collective educational labor for common benefit.
4. Public versus private forms of selfhood: Privatization produces social relations, defined through capitalist reproduction, that function pedagogically to instantiate habits of docility and submission to authority at odds with collective control, dialogue, debate, dissent, and other public democratic practices. Privatization fosters individualization in part by encouraging everyone to understand education as a private service primarily about maximizing one's own capacity for competition. This runs counter to

valuing public schooling for the benefit of all. A new **common school** movement can be involved with producing a new public person imbued with the capacity to recognize and value the collective labor of social life and imagine ways of common benefit from such labor. In both the neoliberal and liberal visions of schooling, the collective labor of teaching and learning aims for accommodation to the existing economic structure and political forms that foster it. Neoliberal capitalism is an economic structure that individualizes benefit from such labor. The task ahead for the critical perspective is to foster the imagining of pedagogical practices, curriculum, and school organization that enact the global commons. How can critical pedagogy make central common labor for common benefit? What path should teachers and students take with communities in recovering control over the work of teaching and learning? How can the struggle against corporate school reform not just be about demanding limits on testing and a cessation to privatization in all its guises but also be about demanding that public education be the basis for reimagining the economy in truly democratic forms, not beholden to purchased and commercialized elections, and reimagining the culture as a public rather than a private one.

Conclusion

Corporate school reform threatens the possibility for public schools to develop as places where knowledge, pedagogical authority, and experiences are taken up in relation to broader political, ethical, cultural, and material struggles informing competing claims to truth. While the battles for critical public schools and against privatization and other manifestations of neoliberalism are valuable struggles in themselves, they should also be viewed as an interim goal to what ought to be the broader goals of developing practices, modes of organizing, and habits of social and self questioning that aim toward the redistribution of state and corporate power from elites to the public while expanding critical consciousness and a radically democratic ethos.

A new common school movement has an inevitably hopeful dimension to it. The common can be built and expanded and it can never be fully enclosed because there are parts of human experience that can't be turned into property and have to be held in common. Compassion, ideas, and the planet itself must be held in common.

Questions for Discussion

1. What were some of the elements of the original common school movement, and how does neoliberal restructuring undermine them?
2. What is enclosure of the commons, and how does enclosure differ from the commons as places for free exchange?
3. What are some of the ways that public control differs from private control of schools, and why does the difference matter for living in common?

Notes

1. See Georges Batailles, *The Accursed Share, Volume One* (New York: Zone Books, 1995). Jean Baudrillard, *The Consumer Society* (Thousand Oaks, CA: Sage, 1998), was an important early work that recognized this while more recently Zygmunt Bauman's *Wasted Lives: Modernity and Its Outcasts* (Polity, 2003), and Henry Giroux's *Youth in a Suspect Society* (New York: Palgrave Macmillan, 2010) make important interventions. Giroux's book significantly links the death of futurity signified in the ramped-up hard and soft war on youth to the dead end of consumer capitalism and ecological disaster.

2. See Richard Wolff's important film *Capitalism Hits the Fan* (2008) produced by Media Education Foundation.

3. Slavoj Zizek, *First as Tragedy, Then as Farce* (New York: Verso, 2009), 91.

4. Zizek, *First as Tragedy*, 91.

5. David Harvey, "The Future of the Commons," *Radical History Review* (Winter 2011): 105.

6. Harvey, "The Future of the Commons," 105.

7. See Linda Darling-Hammond, *The Flat World and Education* (New York: Teachers College Press, 2010) for abundant empirical evidence as to the destructive effects of these anti-teacher policies on the quality of teaching as measured by test outputs.

8. By critically engaged, I am referring not to critical thinking as problem-solving skills but rather critical in the tradition of critical pedagogy, which takes up questions of knowledge in relation to broader power struggles, interests, and social structures.

9. Lois Weiner, *The Global Assault on Teaching, Teachers, and Their Unions* (New York: Palgrave, 2008).

10. See the Bill and Melinda Gates Foundation website, http://www.gatesfoundation.org/college-ready-education/Pages/default.aspx. The Gates website posts a "Featured Fact" that nicely illustrates the assumption that higher education produces economic opportunity: "**Featured Fact:** By 2018, 63 percent of all American job openings will require some sort of postsecondary education." The significance of this "featured fact" is that it suggests that by preparing individuals for higher education, secondary education is creating economic opportunities. This is fallacious in that the education itself does not

create greater levels of employment or effect the unemployment rate or cause expansion or contraction in industries.

http://www.gatesfoundation.org/postsecondaryeducation/Pages/postsecondary-fast-facts.aspx. See also Secretary of Education Arne Duncan's "Call to Service Lecture at Harvard University," available at the U.S. Department of Education website at http://www.ed.gov/news/speeches/call-service-lecture-harvard-university.

11. Arne Duncan put it succinctly shortly before praising the propaganda film *Waiting for Superman*, "As President Obama says, education is one of the best antipoverty programs." Arne Duncan's "Call to Service Lecture at Harvard University," available at the U.S. Department of Education website at http://www.ed.gov/news/speeches/call-service-lecture-harvard-university.

12. Rick Perry claims a Texas miracle in job creation while he was governor, while Mitt Romney said that he created those jobs by luring people from other states to create jobs in Texas (which wouldn't be an option for the U.S. president). An excellent exposé on the state-to-state theft of jobs that are then attributed to elected officials can be found in *This American Life,* episode 435, "How to Create a Job," originally aired May 13, 2011, available online at http://www.thisamericanlife.org/radio-archives/episode/435/how-to-create-a-job.

13. See Edward Herman and Noam Chomsky, *Manufacturing Consent: The Political Economy of the Mass Media* (Pantheon, 2002), and the work of Robert W. McChesney such as *Rich Media, Poor Democracy: Communication Politics in Dubious Times* (New Press, 2000).

ꞓ

Case Studies
Struggles for Critical Education

Case One: Social Justice High School, Little Village Neighborhood, Chicago, Illinois

On May 13, 2001, fourteen parents and community members in this predominantly Mexican American community launched a hunger strike to demand a new high school for their community. After nineteen days the Chicago Public Schools agreed to build the school. The activists maintained their agenda for community control and led the design of the new school.

The result was a campus with four small schools including the Social Justice High School. The school design focused on the relationship between learning and broader social, cultural, and political struggles for justice. The curriculum, animated by the critical pedagogy of Paulo Freire, also emphasized university preparation and one of the campuses focuses on science and mathematics. In 2009 the first students graduated from the school.

Struggles continue over the teacher workforce and the extent to which the community as opposed to the mayor (Commercial Club directed) controls the school. This struggle happened in the context of and despite the radical neoliberal restructuring of the Chicago Public Schools and its aggressive expansion of privatization and chartering, turnarounds, and corporate models of management. This indicates the power of direct action and the possibilities of a small group of dedicated citizens working together to achieve critical pedagogy.

Case Two: Chile, from the "Penguin Revolution" to the "Chilean Winter"

On September 11, 1973, General Augusto Pinochet overthrew the democratically elected government of Chile in a U.S.-backed coup. Widely seen as the first experiment in radical neoliberal restructuring, the dictatorship implemented vast privatization schemes including replacing the public education system with a system of vouchers and privatizing higher education. Even after the restoration of democracy Chile's education system remains mired in this model.

After decades of the consequent financial draining of public school resources and worsened quality, public school students in 2006 initiated the "Penguin Revolution" named for the school uniforms. Students demanded an end to municipal control that limited authoritative public controls and allowed private and public corporations to dominate the public education system. The neoliberal educational policy resulted in dire inequalities that benefited only the rich and hurt everyone else. The 2006 protests included takeovers and occupations of schools and strikes by students that were supported by strikes in multiple sectors.

Many demands of the protesters were met by the government but the Penguins also made challenging neoliberal education a central political issue and set the stage for the Chilean Winter protests of 2011. The Chilean Winter protesters pressed for ending municipal control, reforming the voucher system, implementing public control and public support for secondary and higher education, reforming the admissions process, creating an intercultural university, and a moratorium on the creation of new voucher and charter schools. While progress has been made in forcing the government to restrict for-profit education, the struggle for public education and to overturn the radical neoliberal model continues. The world must learn a lesson from Chile's experience, and Chile's students are teaching it.

Case Three: Porto Allegre, Brazil

Since 1989 the city of Porto Allegre has made critical pedagogy the basis for its education system. The critical approach to curriculum and pedagogy follows the work of Paulo Freire. It extends to a participatory budgeting process. These citizen schools make learning a matter of "reading the world"—linking knowledge to the broader social, political, economic forces and struggles informing it. The process of problem-posing education becomes the basis for community engagement and transformation. The citizen schools are a model of critical pedagogy in action. Scholars and activists from around the world have visited and written about these inspiring successes.

Case Four: Test Refusal in Seattle

Throughout first the George W. Bush and then the Barack Obama administrations, standardized testing has been the basis for a system of financial and autonomy rewards and punishments. Those schools and teachers and students facing the greatest challenges have been punished for test scores while schools, students, and teachers with the greatest privileges have been rewarded for inheriting socially valued knowledge, tastes, and dispositions, that is, cultural capital. Standardized tests are being used not only to justify regressive funding but to attack teacher job security, attack collective bargaining rights, and redefine teacher preparation programs in ways that gut out critical thinking and educational theory, history, and social context.

In the context of high-stakes testing in which schools have had funds cut over scores or been subject to closure and radical untested reforms, teachers, students, and parents have gotten fed up. At the beginning of 2013 Seattle teachers refused to administer the MAP test. Articles in the news media speculated as to the extent to which the Seattle protests will spread. While refusing standardized testing is a hopeful step it is incumbent upon teachers to highlight the cultural politics of the curriculum and the relationship between what is taught and learned and broader social, cultural, political, and economic forces and struggles. It is also crucial for the test refusal movement not to be co-opted by corporate school reformers and used as a basis for holding poorly performing charters and other unproven privatization schemes unaccountable to the public.

Case Five: Chicago Teachers Union Strike

Chicago has endured a century of failed corporate school reforms. The most recent include an aggressive privatization scheme that resulted in firing teachers, opening charter schools, and the proliferation of radical "turnaround" schools. Chicago has been taking the lead at setting the stage for a future two-tiered public system in which the schools of the working class and poor become money-making machines for investors. Within the contracting system money is saved by firing and burning out teachers to keep pay low. Meanwhile the schools of the poorest students on the west and south sides of the city languish in terrible condition.

In the midst of this radical restructuring, the Chicago Teachers Union has been the main obstacle to this contracting scheme. In 2011 Rahm Emanuel, Stand for Children, and other neoliberal groups succeeded in influencing state legislation to restrict the strike capacity of the Chicago Teachers Union. A strike could only be launched with 75 percent of the teachers voting for it. An emboldened Joshua Edelman of Stand for Children bragged on video that the CTU would never be able to strike again. Mayor Rahm Emanuel broke the teachers' contract for annual raises and imposed a longer school day (uncompensated) while promising to close and charter hundreds of schools. Emanuel and the other corporate school reformers waged a relentless teacher- and union-bashing campaign.

The Chicago Teachers Union became the main obstacle to this contracting scheme. Leaders of the Caucus of Rank and File Educators (CORE) Karen Lewis, Jesse Sharkey, Jackson Potter, and others organized the teachers to strike. Chicago teachers nearly unanimously supported the strike, and in September 2012 about 50,000 teachers filled the Chicago loop. The strike was followed in the media globally. What was important and remarkable about the strike was not only winning a favorable contract against the odds and against organized and well-funded hostility and propaganda from business groups and the mayor working for them. It was also that the CORE leadership elevated the strike to highlight the broader political and economic stakes in Chicago's corporate school reform, including issues of poverty, privatization, and de-democratization. The strike inspired many other teachers strikes and became a symbol of teachers' power and resistance in the face of a hostile national climate against unions, public workers, and the very idea of the social good.

Glossary

accommodationist. A perspective that presumes that schooling ought to accommodate the student to the existing social order, political system, economic structure, and dominant culture. Accommodationism tends to mistakenly treat these social systems as relatively fixed and beyond human control rather than recognizing that they are continually produced through human practices. The alternatives to accomodationism are **transformational** perspectives like critical pedagogy and critical theories that assume that schooling ought to be the basis for re-creating social institutions and structures in more just, equal ways.

achievement gap. The difference between mean standardized test scores and the scores of an identified group such as a racial or ethnic minority. In order for a gap to be seen as legitimate, one must accept the dubious premise that the tests and the scores reflect neutral and universally valuable knowledge and culture rather than the knowledge and interests of the groups who made and administer such tests.

adhesion. Paulo Freire's theory of how the oppressed come to see the world through the eyes of the oppressor. For Freire critical pedagogy aims to unveil this false consciousness and illuminate reality so that the student can act to change it. Adhesion involves participating in those ways of seeing and acting that objectify oneself and others. A humanizing pedagogy aims to treat people as subjects.

agency. The sense of one's capacity to act on and shape the social world one inhabits. Different ideological constellations tend to produce different kinds of agency in individuals. Neoliberalism produces a sense of agency defined by social Darwinian competition, selfishness, greed, and pillage of others and the natural world. One can only come to shape the social world as a consumer or a worker in this view. Contrary to this, the tradition of critical pedagogy works to promote in students a sense of agency defined by comprehending the social forces that produce one's experiences such that one can work toward changing those forces. Agency in this tradition is collective rather than individual, social, ethical, and political rather than strictly economic. Henry Giroux, the most significant educational scholar to discuss agency, emphasizes that students learn different senses of agency, which can enable or disable their capacities to interpret what is learned in school and act to shape the forces that produce students' experiences. Students who come from privilege often learn early that they can and ought to act on and shape the world. Oppressed students commonly are taught that their actions and ways of speaking and seeing do not matter to institutions of power.

Althusser, Louis. French Marxist philosopher influenced by Antonio Gramsci and Freudian psychoanalyst Jacque Lacan. His major works include *Lenin and Philosophy*, *Reading Capital*, and *For Marx*. Althusser's essay "Ideology and Ideological State Apparatuses" has been a very important work on reproduction theory.

autonomism. A movement led by Italian Marxists and anarchists emphasizing the expansion of the commons and the increasing centrality of cognitive capital, immaterial labor, and the activities of subjectivity production in the contemporary capitalist economy. Some of the leading autonomists are Antonio Negri, Christian Marrazzi, Franco Berardi, Paulo Virno, Carlos Vercellone, and Nick Dyer-Withford.

autonomy. Rational self-governance; the possibility of living by laws that we create and that we can in turn question, overturn, and re-create.

banking education. A mistaken yet common approach to education in which the student is thought of as an empty vessel to be filled with knowledge or a bank in which knowledge like money is deposited. The metaphor was elaborated by Paulo Freire and describes a view of knowledge as something static that can be delivered rather than a view of knowledge as dynamic that is created through dialogic exchange. The metaphor also describes a view of the person as receiving static knowledge and then instrumentally using this knowledge for self-interested activities. It has no place for comprehending how people have consciousness, how they reflect upon and theorize knowledge, or how knowledge allows one to reconstruct one's experiences and then act on the world through a different understanding. Unfortunately, it is not an exaggeration to say that most educational policy and assessment accepts the poor framing assumptions of banking education. This is why there is such an overemphasis on standardized testing and the standardization of curriculum that aims to deliver and then measure the delivery of knowledge deposited into kids.

Bauman, Zygmunt. Eminent and prolific sociologist from Poland. His scholarship has made significant contributions on the relationship between public and private life, the postmodern condition, globalization, ethics, and consumerism.

biopolitics. A form of politics in which the production and management of life dominates.

Bloom, Allen. Cultural conservative who wrote *The Closing of the American Mind.*

Bourdieu, Pierre. French sociologist and philosopher whose work focused on the relationships between class and culture. He sought to establish the social laws whereby social power was formed, maintained, and passed on. His terms *cultural capital*, *social capital*, and *symbolic violence* have been particularly influential and useful for describing the ways that class hierarchies are reproduced. His book *Social and Cultural Reproduction in Education,* his article by the same name, and his article "The Forms of Capital" have been widely read and cited by critical educators. Bourdieu's work challenges the "human capital" model that has been promoted by Gary Becker and is now largely accepted in which knowledge is seen as a product that directly leads to economic growth.

Bowles, Samuel, and Herbert Gintis. Education thinkers who wrote the book *Schooling in Capitalist America* in 1976. The book had a profound influence on the thinking of left educators in the 1970s and 1980s who shared its concerns with the ways that schools reproduce the labor force and function as a mechanism to reproduce the social order, especially hierarchical class, racial, and gender relationships. Questioning and disagreement with aspects of Bowles and Gintis's thought generated new scholarship on agency, resistance, and culture and education.

canon. A body of literature that is promoted as comprehensive and ought to be mastered by students. Proponents of canon tend to view curriculum as being transmitted. One problem with this view is that it discounts the different power that groups have to determine what goes in and what stays out of the canon. Another problem is that it presumes that knowledge comes from nowhere and is not linked to social interests—as if that which is deemed valuable for others to know does not have to be justified for its value. In other words, canon presumes knowledge to be dogma that ought to be mastered and repeated rather than critically interrogated.

capital. Money or property that is used for investment. Capital in the Marxian tradition is understood as accumulated labor power.

charter schools. Publicly funded but privately managed schools. Some charters are privately managed by for-profit companies. Others are privately managed by nonprofit organizations. Charters began as a grassroots movement initiated by the leader of the American Federation of Teachers, Albert Shanker, and they were intended to inspire experimentation, teacher-led innovation, and the development of new school models. The charter movement has become essentially hijacked by large monied interests with a radically different agenda from the original one. The recent shift has been toward replicating singular school models, getting rid of teachers unions, ending teacher control over schools, and implementing a business-oriented model of test-oriented pedagogy and curricula. The evidence on charters is poor with test scores being on par or worse than neighborhood schools, higher administrative costs, lower teacher pay, worse teacher turnover, and evidence of exacerbated racial segregation. Despite these facts the charter movement is being aggressively promoted by the Gates Foundation and many other neoliberal organizations.

Christian Right. A demographic that consists largely of fundamentalist Christians who share values on creationism in schooling, aspirations to erode the separation of church and state in favor of a religious nation-state, morality understood through religion, a number of conservative views regarding culture (such as censorship) and gender (such as patriarchal assumptions).

common school. The original public school.

confessional technology. A concept of Michel Foucault in which subjects are induced through particular institutions to speak the "truth" of themselves in ways that cohere with domination. What appears as the liberating process of unburdening of the inner authentic contents of the self through confession is in actuality the process of producing oneself as a subject through speaking yet forming oneself in relation to an institution or people in positions of authority—the church, the medical establishment, the psychological establishment, the school, and so on. This is a kind of learned self-regulation and learned submission to authority.

corporate school reformers. Those pursuing the neoliberal agenda of privatization and deregulation in public schooling. Most prominently this includes public school privatization, chartering, vouchers, scholarship tax credits, and expansion of for-profit contracting schemes. This also includes the expansion of the ideology of corporate culture, including standardized testing, so-called data-driven instruction, and other approaches that presume that measurement and control should be central to school reform rather than the emphasis on civic engagement, social renewal, and connecting pedagogy and curriculum to public problems and issues. The expression "corporate school reform" has been widely used by Diane Ravitch who fails to situate it in terms of the broader economic and ideological struggles over neoliberal restructuring.

counterhegemonic. Actions or people who challenge hegemonic power. Because hegemony is held in part through the manufacture of consent, counterhegemonic groups encourage students and others to question the ideologies that give rise to that consent. This struggle is pedagogical in the sense that it involves educating the ideological opposition into the counterhegemonic views.

creative democracy. An expression of philosopher John Dewey from his essay "Creative Democracy: The Task Before Us." Dewey's thought emphasizes the centrality of experience to democratic life and the centrality of schooling for creating the conditions for democratic public life. Dewey concludes that "the task of democracy is forever that of creation of a freer and more humane experience in which all share and to which all contribute."

critical intellectuals. As Giroux elaborates in his book *Teachers as Intellectuals* critical intellectuals are distinguished from transformative intellectuals. Critical intellectuals take up knowledge in relation to questions of power and politics but do not link such analyses to action or foster in students forms of agency that would create conditions for critical knowledge to be transformative.

critical theory. The tradition of thought coming from the Frankfurt School including Theodor Adorno, Max Horkheimer, Herbert Marcuse, Walter Benjamin, Erich Fromm, and Sigfried Kracauer. These social philosophers sought to develop social theory as the basis for social transformation. Critical theory refers more expansively and commonly to an array of left scholarly traditions that include political economy, feminism, postcolonialism, critical mass communications, critical pedagogy, and others. What is shared by these perspectives is a focus on social justice, power relations, struggles against oppression, an attempt to comprehend the relationship between knowledge formations and social power, and an effort to denaturalize oppression that often appears as natural and inevitable.

critical thinking. Problem-solving skills. It is different from **critical theory**, which links claims to truth to matters of ethics, politics, power, and history as part of the project for social transformation.

cultural capital. The knowledge, tastes, and dispositions that are socially valued and systematically rewarded and also the tools of appropriating such knowledge, tastes, and dispositions. Bourdieu distinguished between objectified, embodied, and institutionalized forms of cultural capital. Objectified forms of cultural capital include concrete objects like works of art or books. Embodied cultural capital includes the knowledge, tastes, dispositions, and intellectual modes for appropriating the same. Cultural capital for Bourdieu begins in the home and is rewarded or punished in the schools.

cultural deficit. An assumption of the cultural inferiority of a group and the related belief that such cultural inferiority is responsible for the performance by members of that group on an instrument designed by members of a different cultural group. The group alleging cultural superiority tends to deny its own culture as a culture and usually instead portrays its knowledge, values, and history as universal.

cultural politics of education. Struggles by different groups over meaning-making practices that educate people. The concept of cultural politics as contesting meaning-making practices differs from the idea of culture as a canon or body of knowledge that ought to be formed and preserved and transmitted by cultural elites. The cultural politics of education concerns questions of the struggle over knowledge, curriculum, and pedagogical approaches by different groups with different social positions.

culture wars. The 1980s and 1990s disputes over culture with prominent conservative figures such as Allan Bloom, E. D. Hirsch, and William Bennett arguing for a return to learning classics albeit a select emphasis on some classics rather than others. The culture wars included K–12 school curriculum debates and arguments about higher education. The culture wars were part of the right-wing shift in the United States during the Reagan/Bush era. The conservative culture warriors were nostalgic for the days before the civil rights movement and multiculturalism and particularly resented liberal efforts for cultural inclusion and the displacement of Eurocentrism. Paradoxically the pro-corporate climate in the United States during this period produced a vastly expanded commercialization of culture and in a sense the cultural conservatives were making a last gasp for retaining what conservative economic policies had produced: a culture in which traditional values were replaced by a culture in which everything was for sale. The globalization of corporate media and the advent of a commercially driven twenty-four-hour news cycle played no small part in the transformation that the conservatives reacted against.

curriculum wars. Political disputes over the content of school curriculum. Cultural conservatives tend to promote a canon of the alleged best and brightest texts and perspectives. Liberals tend to argue for adding to this canon history and literature representative of minorities and marginalized groups. Criticalists have sought to displace the canon in favor of comprehending traditions through a central focus on power relations, social justice, ethics, and the politics of claims to the importance of particular texts and traditions.

democracy promotion. The activities of the United States (mainly through USAID) and Europe that are alleged to be about expanding democracy in poorer nations but that critics such as William I. Robinson and Noam Chomsky describe as imperialism or military humanism. These critical views see democracy promotion as a pretext for foreign influence peddling.

determinism. A belief in a force that operates on its own automatically and beyond human intervention. Though determinism can appear in a number of contexts the economy is often falsely viewed through the lens of determinism from various perspectives in a way that naturalizes as inevitable human-made policies and priorities.

Dewey, John. One of the most important American philosophers, the most well-known and read philosopher of education, and a leading thinker behind philosophical pragmatism and progressive education. Dewey's thought emphasized the ethical and political role of education in ongoing social re-creation of democratic society, the centrality of the child, and experience.

disavowal (or denial). Rejection of perceptions because of the traumatic implications of accepting them. For example, many people continue to act as if global warming is not leading to the destruction of the planet because the reality of the destruction of the planet is so traumatic to consider. In this case disavowal becomes part of the process that ensures the realization of the traumatic disaster.

discourse. A group of statements or representations that produce a way of talking about or representing a particular topic in a particular time and place. Discourse defines and makes the objects of our knowledge and informs how ideas are practiced. For Foucault and Derrida nothing meaningful exists outside of discourse. Discourse produces subject positions. Discourse includes signifying (meaning-making) practices, speech acts, and representations that foreground the role of institutions and institutional language.

economism. The reduction of one's understanding of social reality, human culture, and consciousness to economics. This is done on the right by neoliberals who see individuals as primarily self-interested workers and consumers, but it is also done on the left by some Marxists who define human beings by labor and production and treat culture and consciousness as mere effects of economic production.

educational management organizations (EMOs). Companies that contract with districts or schools to privately manage the schools. There are for-profit EMOs and nonprofit EMOs. The for-profit EMO industry is large and is consolidating into fewer large companies. Two of the largest are Edison Learning (formerly the Edison Schools) and K12, Inc., which runs cyber-schools and online homeschooling. The research on test-based performance of these schools is poor. EMOs target those urban and rural schools that have less per-pupil spending and their profits can only come by skimming money out of educational resources. The EMOs cannot get contracts in wealthy school districts because these districts spend up to three times more per pupil ($24,000) than do the EMOs ($8,000). So rich districts would be simply throwing away their public resources and the EMOs would be capturing it as profit.

enclosure. The historical forced transformation of the common pastoral agricultural lands into private property and the related coercion of former inhabitants into wage earner and renters. More recently enclosure has become synonymous with privatization and commodification of public goods and services. Enclosure runs contrary to the expansion of the commons: freely exchanged knowledge, biogenetic information that is the basis of life, and shared physical environment.

Enlightenment. The movement of European thought in the sixteenth through eighteenth centuries that emphasized the use of reason, science, and critical thought in the furtherance of human emancipation, progress, and the public good. See, for example, Immanuel Kant's essay "What Is Enlightenment?". The Enlightenment emerged with the end of the feudal economic era and the rise of capitalism, the decline of monarchy and the rise of parliamentary democracy, and the advent of new technologies for production and discovery. The promise of Enlightenment came to a crisis in the late nineteenth and early twentieth centuries with among other things the development of modern bureaucracy, the human misery of the industrial age, and the coinciding rise of irrationalism in politics with the heights of technological progress.

fatalism. The belief that social outcomes are inevitable and beyond human control. Fatalism is an ideology that encourages people to accept the status quo even though they may be hurt by it.

Ferguson, Ann Arnette. Professor at Smith College and author of *Bad Boys*.

financialization. The shift in capitalism since the advent of neoliberalism in which policy favors the expansion of financial industries and economic leveraging over equity and industrial and agricultural production. Financialization implies an economy in which work becomes dominated by speculating (gambling) as opposed to investing in productive activities. A more biting and honest term that describes financialization is "casino capitalism."

Fordism. The U.S. economy of industrial production in the twentieth century and accompanying forms of self- and social regulation. Fordism involved a view of capital and labor as being partners, a concern of industrial capitalists with the making of consumers who could buy their products and a concern with the life world of the worker beyond the factory floor. Fordism saw the expansion of time and labor-intensive forms of individual and social control that included learned self-management accomplished in various institutions including the public school, psychoanalysis and psychiatry, and social work.

foreign direct investment. The deregulation of nation-state controls over investment by businesses from other nations. This deregulation imposed on poor nations can destroy their local industries when massive foreign companies are allowed to enter their markets.

Foucault, Michel. Influential French philosopher and social theorist of the twentieth century whose work emphasized the relationships between power and knowledge.

Fraser, Nancy. Contemporary critical theorist, a political theorist, and a leading feminist philosopher. Fraser is a professor at the New School for Social Research.

Freire, Paulo. Brazilian educator and social theorist whose most famous book, *Pedagogy of the Oppressed*, formed the groundwork for the educational tradition of critical pedagogy. Freire's thought brings together humanist Marxism, existentialism, postcolonialism, and critical theory. Freire aims for the teacher to lead the student in the vocation of becoming more fully human—that is, to be treated as subjects rather than as objects. This involves praxis to analyze one's own subjective experience in terms of the objective forces that produce it and also to reconstruct one's experience by theorizing it. Such interpretive work then becomes the basis for acting with others to change the social forces that produce the experience.

Gintis, Herbert. *See* **Samuel Bowles**.

Giroux, Henry. American public intellectual and leading figure of critical pedagogy. Giroux's scholarship has made major contributions on educational theory, student resistance, higher education, educational policy and politics, youth, media culture, and race. Giroux's early work focused on theorizing schooling and student and teacher resistance. In the early 1990s his work shifted and expanded to focus on cultural politics in education, mass media, and art. He became the leading thinker on the relationship between education and culture. At the turn of the millennium Giroux became increasingly focused on neoliberalism, the assault on the public sphere, violence, and the rise of authoritarianism while remaining engaged in many areas. Theoretically Giroux's work is informed by and draws from a number of traditions including philosophical pragmatism, poststructuralism, structuralism, postcolonialism, race studies, and feminism.

global governance. The political interaction and influence of transnational actors. The concept allows a way of comprehending nonstate sovereignty waged by organizations that span nation-states. The World Trade Organization for example represents multinational corporations and is not restricted to a single nation yet it influences the policies and actions of multiple nations.

Gramsci, Antonio. Italian philosopher, political activist, and social theorist whose most famous writings, *The Prison Notebooks,* were written while he was imprisoned by Benito Mussolini. Gramsci's theory of hegemonic change, which emphasized cultural struggle in civil society, and his theory of intellectuals have been influential in a number of academic traditions including critical education including the work of Henry Giroux and Michael Apple and in cultural studies.

Guantanamo Bay. Detention camp is located within the United States Guantanamo Naval Base in Cuba. It is notorious for harsh treatment of prisoners, torture alleged by both Red Cross inspectors and former inmates, and holding suspected terrorists indefinitely thereby defying the right of habeas corpus.

Hall, Stuart. Jamaican British professor who led the development of cultural studies across numerous disciplines. He was influenced by Raymond Williams and E. P. Thompson and went on to educate a number of influential cultural theorists. Cultural studies developed in the 1980s and peaked in its influence in the late 1990s. Hall brought together critical theory, Gramsci, Foucault, semiotics, continental philosophy, postcolonialism, race studies, and feminism.

Hanushek, Erik. Right-wing economist of education who regularly makes arguments for treating schooling as a private consumable commodity and frames the social uses of education for business.

hegemony. A dominant power. The term can also refer to the struggle for ascendancy by different competing groups. The latter definition elaborated by Gramsci is important for education because it is education that allows different groups to win other groups over by articulating common sense and defining the terms of the culture.

Hirsch, E. D. English professor who has become most well known for championing the conservative cultural canon and promoting the idea that every student ought to know the same things. Hirsch more recently has been an investor in K12, Inc., a for-profit online charter school and homeschooling company. Profit is made in the charter schools by reducing the number of teachers and increasing class sizes. Standardized test performance among students of these schools tends to be worse than district averages. Studies of cyberschools reveal them to do even worse than the majority of charters in traditional test-based measures.

Hoover Institution. A right-wing think tank that in education promotes business interests over the public interest, neoliberal privatization and deregulation, and anti-unionism.

ideological state apparatus. A term developed by Louis Althusser in his essay "Ideology and Ideological State Apparatuses" that refers to institutions that promote the dominant state ideology. Althusser laid out a Marxist Lacanian theory of education as a major site of ideological subject formation. The essay explains that ideology is the process of making subjects through practices and that this is accomplished in institutions. There are two kinds of institutions: repressive state apparatuses that work to reproduce the class order mostly through coercion, and ideological state apparatuses that do so through manufacturing consent. Althusser explains that schools are the dominant ideological state apparatus, teaching skills and know-how in ways that produce social relationships conducive to the reproduction of labor relations. This theory of ideology emphasizes the *materiality* of ideology as being produced through rituals and practices and that ideology represents the *imaginary* relationship of the subject to the production process.

interpellation. A theory of identity formation that is simultaneously an explanation of ideology. Interpellation is a process of being hailed or called by a dominant institution. In the process of being recognized, one recognizes oneself as a subject of the institution and simultaneously as subject to the institution. Althusser gives the example of the policeman yelling, "Hey, you!" and in the act of turning to respond to the call one is hailed or made as an ideological subject. One is both made into a subject of ideology and made subject to authority of the institution calling one. The same process would hold for the teacher calling on the student. The limitation of the theory of interpellation is that it does not allow for the ways that individuals resist being made into a subject, how they have complicated and contradictory consciousness, and how people can be re-educated into being subjects who might radically criticize the existing order and who can work with others to make a different order.

inverted totalitarianism. A form of authoritarianism that is enacted through a system of corporate domination of the state, production of political apathy among the population, and a "managed democracy" in which money dominates political institutions and politics becomes a performance. Sheldon Wolin coined the term to distinguish it from the traditional totalitarianism of fascist regimes.

K12, Inc. One of the two biggest for-profit private schooling companies. K12, Inc. is unique in that it is an online format. About half of its customers are homeschoolers and the rest are cyberschools. The curriculum is culturally conservative having been informed by E. D. Hirsch and William Bennett who are investors and high-profile right-wing culture warriors. Profit is made by minimizing teachers and their salaries and relying on mass-produced lessons and low-paid teachers. Test scores for K12 schools are weak relative to neighborhood schools.

magnet schools. Public schools that are able to select some portion of their student body and often draw high-testing students out of neighborhood schools. Magnet schools began as an effort at racial equity aiming to racially integrate districts. During the Reagan administration they were reinvented by the political right to justify privatization schemes. A major effect of magnet schools in major cities is to supply professional-class parents with school catering to their children who tend to have more cultural capital. Another effect is to skim working-class students with high test scores from neighborhood schools, thereby lowering the test performance of the neighborhood schools and segregating schools by academic performance and class.

Mann, Horace. The founder of the common school movement, which became the basis for the public school system.

market fundamentalism. A belief in markets and business as the model and solution for all social and individual problems, also known as neoliberalism. Market fundamentalists champion privatization and deregulation and see individuals as primarily consumers and workers while dismissing collective values.

McKinsey Consultants. A management consulting company that has had a prominent role in advising governments and school districts to take a private sector approach (including privatization and corporate-style management) to public sector reform.

Milken, Michael. The founder of K12, Inc., one of the two largest private schooling companies. Milken was a junk bond trader in the 1980s until he was convicted of fraud and insider trading and served prison time. Upon release he was barred from trading in the financial industry, and he turned to education entrepreneurship. He rapidly built one of the largest for-profit education companies by buying up smaller education companies.

modes of identification. The ways in which individuals identify with particular roles or positions.

monetarist policy. The management of money supplies by the Federal Reserve to keep inflation low while attempting to stimulate economic expansion. Monetarism is associated with neoliberal economist Milton Friedman.

multiculturalism. A grassroots movement that began in the 1970s that sought to recognize the cultures of different groups in K–12 curriculum and in higher education. Liberal multiculturalism focusing on cultural recognition and expanding the canon to include marginalized cultures and figures dominated the educational discourse through the 2000s. But some educators, notably

Christine Sleeter, Peter McLaren, Henry Giroux, Donaldo Macedo, and Pepi Leistyna, promoted a critical multiculturalism that linked the recognition of cultural differences to broader power struggles and social structures.

neoliberalism. An economic doctrine that calls for privatizing public goods and services, deregulating government controls over capital, and encouraging trade deregulation. As a cultural ideology neoliberalism encourages people to think in terms of individual gain as opposed to public interest. Neoliberals tend to see the role of the state as furthering the interests of businesses and owners, maintaining the repressive institutions of the society, and destroying the caregiving institutions of the society. Neoliberalism is especially associated with deregulation, such as the deregulation of Wall Street and the housing and automotive industries that resulted in the economic crises of the 2000s and the need for public sector bailout. As a cultural ideology, neoliberalism seeks to disguise the role that public support plays in private sector wealth, for example in the form of infrastructure (roads, schools, and the like) that make private sector activity possible. Critics of neoliberalism like David Harvey see it as a form of class warfare in which the wealthy seek to redistribute wealth and resources upwardly (to those few at the top) while educating everyone to see the world through the lens of financial elites.

neovouchers. *See* **scholarship tax credits.**

object (of history). A self-conception that one is only acted on by forces beyond one's control. Fatalistic pedagogies treat students as objects, as does banking education.

official knowledge. The knowledge in curriculum and pedagogy that represents dominant ideology or ruling-class and group interests and perspectives. This expression is found developed most in Michael Apple's work, particularly the book *Ideology and Curriculum*. The concept draws on the scholarship relating class and culture as elaborated by Raymond Williams and Pierre Bourdieu.

organic intellectuals. Intellectuals who emerge from within a group's own social position, interests, and values. Groups that can cultivate organic intellectuals tend to succeed in conflict with other groups.

panopticon. A prison design by British utilitarian philosopher Jeremy Bentham in which a watchtower is surrounded by a circular configuration of prison cells. The design allowed for fewer guards because the prisoners did not know whether they were being watched at any given moment. Foucault uses the idea of the panopticon to explore the modern technology of power that he terms "hierarchical surveillance."

Pearson NCS. The largest educational publishing company. They are involved in numerous for-profit endeavors from textbook publishing to test-making to curriculum design. For criticism of their educational influence see Stephen Ball's *Global Education, Inc.*

performativity. The way in which gender is created through performance and discourse that is historically dependent. Every time we speak or act, we reproduce the norms of gender, but we also change it slightly by giving it a designation it did not have before we embodied it.

political economy. The analysis of economic production, buying, selling, and money in a state or between states. Historically, political economy predated the modern discipline of economics, counting Adam Smith and Karl Marx among its ranks. Originally political economy was a branch of moral philosophy. Political economists today, especially from the Marxist or critical tradition, tend to be concerned with the social, ethical, political, and symbolic dimensions of economic concepts or assumptions continuing its heritage in moral philosophy.

political liberalism. An Enlightenment philosophy that embraces equality and liberty. Liberalism has tended to support electoral democracy and rule of law, civil right, press freedom, freedom of religion, free and fair elections as well as free trade and private property. Liberalism broke with prior tendencies toward hereditary privilege, monarchy, state religion, and divine right of kings.

political subjectivities. Senses of self defined by political identification, values, and vision for the future.

portfolio model. A view of education that likens the management of schools to stock investment. In the portfolio model, the superintendent is imagined as a stock investor and schools are imagined as stocks in a portfolio (district). The portfolio model promotes the idea that public schooling should be contracted out to private companies and that the schools that succeed should be kept open while the schools that don't should be allowed to "go out of business." This is referred to as "churn" or "creative destruction." The advocates of the portfolio model such as Paul T. Hill admit that there is no way to measure the success of the portfolio model in terms of test scores improvements. Hill suggests that the success of the model should be measured by the extent to which more schools are subject to the model.

positivist ideology. A belief that truth must be numerically quantifiable and that subjective experiences must be denied in the pursuit of objective truth. Positivism is reflected in the push for standardized testing in which the values of those making the tests are presented as objective truth that all students must naturally master.

post-Fordism. The era of the late twentieth and early twenty-first centuries that has seen U.S. manufacturing move overseas and domestic work shift to service labor. Post-Fordism involves a belief that individuals must solely provide for their own social welfare, an emphasis on entrepreneurship, and the commodification of the public sector in the form of for-profit prison and schools.

poststructuralism. An intellectual movement that sought to elucidate the discontinuities, ruptures, and differences at the core of the self, the society, and regimes of truth. Poststructuralist thinkers such as Michel Foucault and Jacques Derrida challenged the tenets of structuralism, which sought to ascertain the social laws, inertia, and continuities accounting for social phenomena such as De Saussure's structural linguistics, Levi-Strauss's structural anthropology, and Bourdieu's sociology. Poststructuralism tends to focus on language, difference, and the local, rejecting what Lyotard referred to as "grand narratives" inherited from the Enlightenment such as emancipation, progress, and Truth.

praxis. Reflective action in which one theorizes experience and uses the insights to inform future action. Praxis joins theory and practice toward the end of social transformation.

preferred meaning. The meaning that a representation tends to take within a particular cultural context. While representations are radically indeterminate and open to different meanings they tend to be interpreted in specific ways in particular social and historical moments. Stuart Hall uses the term as part of his constructivist theory of culture. It challenges the idea that meanings of cultural representations are radically indeterminate and everyone's interpretation is equally possible and it challenges the assumption that representations are determined and guaranteed by the intention of the cultural producer.

privatization. The transfer of ownership and control of public, collectively owned resources to individual private ownership and control.

public sphere. The discursive space opened up by the public exchange of speech. The public sphere addresses public problems such that collective political action can be taken. The public sphere is distinct from the private sphere of economic exchange and civil society and also distinct from the state.

radical democracy. A critical political theory developed most by Ernesto Laclau and Chantal Mouffe in *Hegemony and Socialist Strategy* and by Mouffe in *The Return of the Political* and *The Democratic Paradox*. David Trend's edited collection *Radical Democracy* brings together a number of major contemporary thinkers on the topic. Radical democracy reimagines socialism through a cultural focus indebted to Derridaean deconstruction and American pragmatism. It attempts to displace class as the sole or central political identity. Radical democracy presumes that society is structured through antagonism and seeks to overcome the limitations of liberal pluralism's emphasis on consensus and denial of difference.

resistance. The ways that opposition to domination can be theorized and become the basis for collective action against oppressive forces. Acts of opposition do not on their own amount to resistance.

return of the repressed. The tendency of the unconscious to refuse repression and for repressed desires and drives to break through to consciousness. Frederic Nietzsche's philosophy (see, for example, *Twilight of the Idols*) offered a social return of the repressed in his discussion of how the modern emphasis on positivity effaces darkness and difference, which cannot be contained. This prefigured the Frankfurt school of critical theory's version of return of the repressed in *Dialectic of Enlightenment*, the uncontainable energy of the planet found in Georges Bataille's *Accursed Share*, and more recent postmodern/poststructural versions such as the theme of haunting found in Derrida.

scholarship tax credits (neovouchers). State tax credits that citizens are given to encourage them to opt out of public schools and instead use the credit for private schooling. The Walton Family Foundation is a major promoter of this privatization scheme.

school vouchers. A credit for private schooling that is paid by the public school system. Proponents claim vouchers allow citizens to shop for schools and that this forces schools to compete for customers. Critics cite the defunding of public schools, the low quality of much private schooling, and the use of vouchers for religious education. Chile has had one of the most extensive and destructive experiments with vouchers, but a massive public push-back has scaled back the use of vouchers there. The use of vouchers has had poor results in several U.S. cities including D.C., New Orleans, and Milwaukee. Despite the lack of evidence vouchers have recently been expanded statewide by Republican politicians in Wisconsin, New Jersey, Louisiana, and Michigan. The Walton Family Foundation (of the Wal-Mart fortune) has been the largest promoter of voucher schemes in the United States.

signifying practices. Meaning-making practices like language, gestures, and action that create meaning within a particular context. Imagine the student putting his head down on the desk or throwing the desk or walking out of class. These actions require interpretation. Do they describe illness, oppositional behavior, or political resistance?

social capital. The social networks that individuals are able to join that allow for certain privileges. For example, those with the right social connections may game the selective enrollment process in cities that have competitive entrance to the top public schools or have contacts who help them manipulate public and private systems to their advantage.

social character. Those character traits that members of a society hold in common. The term was developed by critical theorist and psychoanalyst Erich

Fromm in, for example, "Character and the Social Process" in *Escape from Freedom*. He explains that social character develops from basic experience and mode of life. The concept explains why some ideas fall flat and others take powerful hold in particular cultures at particular times. Social character internalizes external necessities harnessing human energy for a given economic and social system.

social construction. An approach to culture emphasizing the extent to which material things (including bodies) are only meaningful through historically constituted relations of difference and distinction. Social construction challenges claims to the naturalness and fixity of identity categories.

social Darwinism. An ideology in which Darwinian evolution is applied to society and politics to suggest that survival-of-the-fittest competition is best for everyone. It tends to justify deeply inegalitarian social policies, falsely positioning such policies as justified by nature.

social relations of resistance. Relationships between people defined by oppressed people resisting oppression and domination.

subject (of history). The understanding that a person can act rather than simply be acted upon. Oppression results from people treating others as objects rather than as human subjects. The aim of critical pedagogy is to help people understand their oppression so they may become actor/subjects rather than objects. For Paulo Freire, this is the process of humanization.

subject position. Michel Foucault's conception of the subject as being produced by discourse. Individuals are not subjects who produce knowledge; rather people occupy subject positions that are produced discursively.

symbolic violence. The devaluation of one's culture, knowledge, language, tastes, and dispositions. In education, symbolic violence involves the student internalizing the "rules of the game" such as the valuing of professional-class values over working-class values. In a context of symbolic violence, a working-class student may learn to judge herself as inferior, lazy, and undeserving of social reward. The student is thus made complicit in her own cultural oppression. Pierre Carles's film about Pierre Bourdieu, "Sociology is a Martial Art," illustrates the power and reach of symbolic violence. The film begins and ends with a very moving scene of Bourdieu about to give one of his last lectures to a Chicago audience by videoconference from the French hospital where he was dying of cancer. Bourdieu, who grew up working class, fidgets nervously before the camera and finally laughs and explains that he is terribly nervous to speak in English, a foreign tongue. He then says that this nicely exemplifies "linguistic insecurity.w" Here is the most important living sociologist made to feel fear as he is subject to the English language, the language of power of the U.S. academy. Of course, for regular working-class people the language of power in numerous institutions subjects them to symbolic violence.

theory. Rational, contemplative, or speculative abstract thought. In education, theory is often falsely posed as at odds with practice. In reality all practices have theoretical assumptions underpinning them. Theory invites teachers and other cultural producers to explore the assumptions that inform their practices and to rework their experiences toward better practices.

Tooley, James. A British academic who has become well known for promoting fee-for-service for-profit schooling in poor nations that lack universal public education. Tooley's work has been embraced by the World Bank, but it has been criticized for promoting market-based rather than free universal and public schooling. Tooley has also been extensively criticized for writing a book against feminism and gender equality.

trade liberalization. The removal of tariffs and limits to the movement of capital and goods across borders. Trade liberalization shifts control of trade away from nation-states and the citizens and workers they represent to private parties who own industry.

traditional intellectuals. Intellectuals who claim to be doing disinterested work yet produce knowledge in the service of the ruling groups.

transformative intellectuals. Intellectuals who both link knowledge to power and politics and foster action and political agency.

venture philanthropy. Charitable giving modeled on venture capital. The largest venture philanthropists are the Gates, Broad, and Walton foundations. Venture philanthropy promotes privatization and the modeling of schooling on private, for-profit corporations. The public forgoes tax revenue by allowing private individuals to give to philanthropies and then the large venture philanthropies are able to use their size and wealth to dominate policy making. The public essentially pays to give away control over public resources such as schools.

vouchers. *See* **school vouchers; scholarship tax credits.**

Weiner, Lois. A scholar of critical education whose focus includes teachers unions, teacher education, and globalization and education.

welfare state. Governments and nations with strong social safety net programs. The United States created governmental safety nets in the wake of the Great Depression in the 1930s that were expanded in the Great Society reforms of the 1960s. These programs mitigated the extreme effects of capitalism and thereby helped countless people who would otherwise have lacked housing, food, shelter, and medical care. The conservative shift of the Reagan era scaled back the welfare state, and the Clinton administration continued that trend through its welfare reform legislation. Welfare was transformed into punishing "workfare" programs that underpaid the poor for required work, and much public housing was privatized. The corporate media and politicians have since made the term "welfare" a pejorative term rather than associating it with virtuous care for those in need.

Whittle, Christopher. The founder of Edison Schools, one of the first and largest for-profit private school companies. Whittle started his career as an advertiser and subsequently created Channel One, a for-profit cable channel that marketed educational programing interspersed with ads to school districts. As the founder of Edison Schools (now Edison Learning) Whittle sought to profit from the discrepancy between what a school district paid the company per pupil and what the company spent per pupil. He achieved this by keeping as profit the amount that otherwise would be going for teacher pay, smaller class sizes, and more books and resources. Edison targets poor communities that have the least to spend per pupil. More recently Whittle opened a for-profit private school called Avenues, and he has said he plans to use the school brand to create knock-off educational products targeting students in poor countries.

Zizek, Slavoj. Slovenian philosopher and cultural theorist whose work draws principally from Hegel, Lacan, and Marx. His books engage contemporary political and philosophical problems frequently through popular culture such as film.

Index

About the Author

Kenneth J. Saltman is professor of educational policy studies and research where he teaches in the Social and Cultural Foundations of Education graduate program at DePaul University. He is the author of numerous books including most recently of *The Failure of Corporate School Reform* (Paradigm, 2012); *Toward a New Common School Movement* (Paradigm, 2013) with Noah De Lissovoy and Alex Means; and *Neoliberalism, Education, and Terrorism* (Paradigm, 2013) with Jeffrey Di Leo, Henry Giroux, and Sophia McClennen. His prior two books, *The Gift of Education: Public Education and Venture Philanthropy* (Palgrave, 2010), and *Capitalizing on Disaster: Taking and Breaking Public Schools* (Paradigm, 2007), received American Education Studies Association Critics Choice book awards. He is a recipient of a Fulbright Chair in Globalization and Culture, Associate Editor of Journal of Education Policy, and fellow of the National Education Policy Center.